The Ten Dimensions (

The Ten Dimensions of Inclusion

Non-Catholic Students in Catholic Schools

James Kent Donlevy
University of Calgary, Canada

SENSE PUBLISHERS
ROTTERDAM/BOSTON/TAIPEI

A C.I.P. record for this book is available from the Library of Congress.

ISBN 978-90-8790-805-8 (paperback)
ISBN 978-90-8790-806-5 (hardback)
ISBN 978-90-8790-807-2 (e-book)

Published by: Sense Publishers,
P.O. Box 21858, 3001 AW
Rotterdam, The Netherlands
http://www.sensepublishers.com

Printed on acid-free paper

This book is dedicated to my girls, Kaitlyn and Shayne. It was because of them that I became interested in the phenomenon of inclusion and twelve years later they continue to inspire and bless me in so many ways. It is also dedicated to my friend and mentor Dr. Keith Walker, a professor at the University of Saskatchewan, a man of conscience and wisdom who prepared me to write my dissertation and thus this book. He is a Man for All Seasons.

TABLE OF CONTENTS

PREFACE

GENESIS & DEFINITION

This book has been in development since 1998 when I first experienced the phenomenon of non-Catholic students in Catholic schools in the Canadian province of Saskatchewan. My daughters were attending a Catholic high school and it struck me that I had not noticed their friends attending Sunday Mass. Upon inquiry, I discovered that many of their friends were not Catholics and that in my youngest daughter's words "It really doesn't make a difference Dad. They are my friends." Well that was fine except I suspected that the demographics of Catholic schools which I had attended had changed. I wondered if my understanding was correct and further, if so, what were the effects of such a demographic change in the religion of some of the student body in Catholic schools? It was with those thoughts in mind that in 2000 I chose the topic "Catholic Education and the Inclusion of Non-Catholic Students: Qualitative Findings and Implications" for my doctoral dissertation. Since that time I have been researching, reading, and writing on the topic of the inclusion of non-Catholic students in Catholic schools. It has been a fascinating study into the various aspects of Catholic schools which have been touched by the phenomenon of non-Catholic inclusion which I refer to in this book as inclusion.

After several years of research, it became very clear that there were many aspects of inclusion which were symbiotic and inter-related. Indeed, ten dimensions of the phenomenon emerged from the readings, research, and writing which I have experienced during my years of research. I first wrote on that finding in an article published in *Catholic Education: A Journal of Inquiry and Practice.* It was the writing of that article, along with subsequent research which produced further academic articles, which brought me to the writing of this book. This book is an amalgam of the findings from my research.

SIGNIFICANCE

The significance of inclusion is clear. The Canadian Catholic Schools Trustees' Association (2006) notes that inclusion has become a major issue in Saskatchewan as public school districts seek financial compensation for non-Catholic students attending Catholic schools. In Alberta, litigation has commenced involving the financial loss to the Public school district due to non-Catholic students attending an expanded Catholic school district (Board of Trustees of Aspen View Regional Division No. 19, n.d.). In Ontario, the Ontario Catholic School Trustees Association (2000) identified what they believed to be one of the "Major Issues Facing Catholic Education . . . the increasing number of non-Catholic students who are present in the secondary schools . . ." (p. 17). Dixon (2003) noted that in six dioceses in Ontario, the non-Catholic student population varied from 10% to 50%.

In the United States the average number of non-Catholic students in Catholic schools is approximately 13.5 percent. I presented a paper on the topic of inclusion at the 2003 National Catholic Educational Association's Convention in St. Louis and was advised that the topic is of increasing concern to Catholic schools in America.

In 1980 it was noticed in the United States that the evangelization of non-Catholic students in Catholic schools (Schillo, 1980) was an issue and, in Canada in 1999, Mulligan raised the issue of inclusion stating that it "is a concern common to Catholic educators in Ontario, Saskatchewan and Alberta" (p. 182). He reiterates some of the concerns of others (Dixon, 2003) in offering four reasons for this difficulty: a) the mission of the Catholic school is to evangelize Catholic students, not to persuade non-Catholic students to join the Faith; b) school policies require non-Catholic students to accept all Catholic dimensions of the school programs in order to discourage attendance by non-Catholics for mere reasons of convenience; c) evangelization is not school-wide nor all inclusive as non-Catholic students can not receive the sacraments; and d) religion teachers are hindered in their religious mission as,

> How can a teacher, in the same religion class, help students who have an active faith to grow in knowledge and deepen in commitment; try to help the unchurched Catholic students to discover new meaning in the church and faith they have definite but tenuous ties to; and respect a significant number of students for whom Catholic faith is a foreign language that they have no, or next to no, interest in learning about (p. 183)?

With respect to the evangelization of non-Catholic students a brief aside comment is warranted. Throughout this book the position taken is that the evangelization of non-Catholic students is not a goal of the Catholic school. However, the General Directory for Catechesis (Congregation for the Clergy, 1997) seems to suggest that non-Catholic students may be evangelized at least by implication as a result of being present within the wider group of Catholic students in the Catholic school. The Congregation says,

> When most students attending a Catholic school belong to families who associate themselves with the school because of its Catholic character, the ministry of the word can be exercised in it in multiple forms: primary proclamation, scholastic religious instruction, catechesis, homily. Two of these forms, however, have a particular importance in the Catholic school: religious instruction in the school and catechesis whose respective characteristics have already been discussed. (271) When students and their families become associated with Catholic schools because of the quality of education offered in the school, or for other possible reasons, catechetical activity is necessarily limited and even religious education—when possible—accentuates its cultural character. The contribution of such schools is always "a service of great value to men", (272) as well as an internal element of evangelization of the Church. Given the plurality of socio-cultural and

religious contexts in which the work of Catholic schools is carried on in different nations, it is opportune that the Bishops and the Episcopal Conferences specify the kind of catechetical activity to be implemented in Catholic schools. (para. 260)

Jelinski (1994) found similar concerns among the Canadian province of Saskatchewan's Catholic school administrators. He examined the procedures, practices, and policies for admission into Saskatchewan's Catholic schools and noted the comments of in-school administrators regarding the perceived difficulties associated with the admission of non-Catholic students. Among those comments: if the number of non-Catholic students is too great, the reason for existing as a Catholic school is destroyed; the addition of non-Catholic students to non-practicing Catholic students put a heavy burden on Catholic teachers; the watering down of Catholic teachings to accommodate others weakens the Catholic schools' reason for existing; once non-Catholic students are admitted they never get reevaluated to determine if they should remain in the system; younger children don't feel part of the sacramental preparation process and it can be traumatic for them (pp. 50–54).

In the United Kingdom there has been recent concern over a Ministerial suggestion that faith based schools, which includes Catholic schools, should – under a Schools Admissions Code – be required to have a minimum of 25% of their students from outside of the school's faith group (Bogle, 2007; see also School Admissions Code of Practice, February 2003, section 3.10).

In Ireland, the government has determined the necessity of funding non-Catholic schools for immigrants (International Herald Tribune: Europe, Dec. 13, 2007) and in January 2008, "The Archdiocese of Dublin . . . announced a new admissions policy for 2 parochial schools, reserving one-third of the available seats for non-Catholic students" (Catholic World News, January 23, 2008, p.1).

In Australia, the issue of inclusion remains a current issue in Catholic schools (Catholic News, April 8, 2005). In 2007, the Catholic School Enrollments Trend indicated that there were "170,000 non-Catholic students enrolled in Australian Catholic schools, which represented 25% of all students. . . [and] that the proportion of non-Catholic enrolments ranged from 20% in NSW to 44% in Tasmania" (National Catholic Education Commission, 2008). Inclusion remains a concern (Bishops of New South Wales and the ACT, 2007; Harkness, n.d.).

As an aside, the presence of non-Catholic students in Catholic schools in Canada has also triggered a desire on the part of some non-Catholic parents to become members of the Catholic school boards in at least one Canadian Catholic school system. The Supreme Court of the North West Territories (Yellowknife Catholic Schools v. Euchner, 2007) has recently affirmed the right of non-Catholic citizens to sit as Catholic school Trustees. Although this decision seems restricted to those provinces which do not have constitutionally protected Catholic schools, as in the Provinces of Ontario, Alberta, and Saskatchewan, it is still a concern for the future of Canada's Catholic schools in other provinces and territories and what that may portend for the public's acceptance of Catholic school boards in the three aforesaid provinces.

In sum, the inclusion of non-Catholic students in Catholic schools is a topic whose time has come in Canada and as Francis (1986) suggested in the United Kingdom, "the place of non-Catholic pupils in Catholic secondary schools is a proper subject for educational research" (p. 1).

BOOK OUTLINE OF CHAPTERS

This book draws upon my understanding and findings from four qualitative studies conducted by me within two Canadian provinces as well as an amalgam of relevant documents of the Catholic Church, the academic writings of others, and media reports. It is from those sources that I have attempted to shed some light on the phenomenon of the inclusion of non-Catholic students within 10 dimensions: social/cultural, political, financial, legal, racial, administrative, pedagogical, psychological, spiritual, and philosophical. The data from theses four studies is from constitutionally protected and funded Catholic high schools. The other sources of data are both national (Canadian) and international. Therefore, this book should be read with those delimitations in mind. I will be among the first to acknowledge that there may be more dimensions to be yet identified, but I leave that to others in the field.

This book is composed of a Preface, Introduction, and eleven Chapters. The Preface briefly describes the significance of the phenomenon to Catholics in Canada, the United States, the United Kingdom, and Australia. The Introduction provides the foundations for the book with a review of the Catholic Church's view of inclusion as stated in Vatican documents, the data provided by scholars, statements on the topic within the media, and the methodology and methods which I employed in examining the phenomenon in four studies.

Chapter 1 looks to the first dimension of inclusion, the social/cultural aspects of the phenomenon. In particular, the chapter draws upon the research and looks at inclusion from the perspectives of Catholic teachers, Catholic students, and non-Catholic students. It then moves onto the theoretical aspects of how the common good is addressed by inclusion from the perspectives of Liberalism and Communitarianism.

Chapter 2 provides the second dimension: the political ramifications of the phenomenon. The social contract between Catholics and the public is seen under pressure due to the political debates in Ontario and Saskatchewan regarding the reasons for Catholic schools.

Chapter 3 states the financial aspects of inclusion in Ontario, Saskatchewan, and Alberta. In particular, the issue of the cost of the public funding of Catholic schools as well as the difficulties facing some public school boards where non-Catholic students attend Catholic schools – allegedly enticed to do so by those schools.

Chapter 4 examines the legal aspects of inclusion. This rather lengthy chapter sets out the constitutional foundation for Catholic schools in Ontario, Saskatchewan, and Alberta and moves onto the implications for non-Catholic students' rights under the Canadian Charter of Rights and Freedoms. Further, consideration is given to the legal conundrum facing Catholic school districts in Alberta who wish to expand their school districts into what has been public school districts.

Chapter 5 offers the fifth dimension, racial; and it notes the rise in the number of Islamic students in Ontario's urban Catholic schools and the increase in First Nations students in Saskatchewan's schools. Further, mention is made of how race has played a role in the Catholic school's approach to inclusion as viewed from the literature.

Chapter 6 provides research into the administrative aspects of inclusion and notes, amongst other things, the importance of the Catholic school principal's initial interview with non-Catholic parents and their children when the latter seek admission to the Catholic school.

Chapter 7 looks to the pedagogical aspects of inclusion. In particular, Chapter 7 examines the difficulty of providing catechesis to non-Catholic students and the relationship between non-Catholic students and Catholic teachers. Further, the issue of balancing orthodoxy and orthopraxis in the schools with respect to all of the students is addressed.

Chapter 8 delves into the psychology of inclusion, as that term is defined in this book. Specifically, it looks at the psychological impact of inclusion as understood by Catholic teachers, Catholic students, and non-Catholic students.

Chapter 9 proffers a glimpse into the spiritual aspect of inclusion insofar as Catholic spirituality differs markedly from secular spirituality and why that distinction is significant for inclusion.

Chapter 10 moves to perhaps the most difficult dimension of inclusion – the philosophical dimension. It is quite complex as it deals with the philosophical implications of inclusion, in particular the impact of that phenomenon on Catholic teachers, Catholic students, and non-Catholic students. It further considers the difficulty involved with the Catholic Church's understanding of conscience and how that arguably impacts the relationships of teachers and school administrators with non-Catholic students.

Chapter 11 provides some final thoughts on the future of inclusion within Canada's constitutionally protected Catholic schools and how that might be best achieved, not only for those students and for Catholic education, but the common good in Canadian society.

It is important to acknowledge that this book is a compilation and crystallization of my work done in the area of the inclusion of non-Catholic students into Catholic schools which has been underway since 1998. In that respect, the following journals have kindly allowed for the re-publication of much of the text of my past papers in this book.

1. Donlevy, J. K. (2002). Catholic Schools and Open Boundaries: The Inclusion of Non-Catholic students.
   Canadian Journal of Education (2002) 27/1.

2. Donlevy, J. K. (2004). Value Pluralism and Negative Freedom: The Surrey and Trinity Cases.
   McGill Journal of Education 39 (3) pp. 305–32.

3. Donlevy, J.K. (2005) Re-Visiting Denominational Cause and Denominational Breach in Canada's Constitutionally Protected Catholic Schools.
   Journal of Education and Law. Vol. 15, 3, pp. 85–112.

4. Donlevy, J.K. (2006). Non-Catholic Students Impact Upon Catholic Students in Four Catholic High Schools.
   Journal of Religion and Society, Vol. 8.

5. Donlevy, J.K. (2007). Non-Catholic Students Impact on Catholic Teachers in Four Catholic High Schools
   Religious Education. Vol. 102, Is. 1 pp. 4–24.

6. Donlevy, J.K. (2007) Ten Dimensions of Inclusion: Non-Catholic students in Catholic Schools.
   Catholic Education: A Journal of Inquiry and Practice. Vol. 10, No. 3. pp. 293–320.

7. Donlevy, J.K. (2008.). The Common Good: Catholic Schools and the Inclusion of Non-Catholic Students
   Journal of Beliefs and Values: Studies in Religion and Education .Vol. 29, No. 2, 161–171. [United Kingdom.]

8. Donlevy, J. K. (2008, February). Catholic Schools and Freedom of Conscience in the Canadian Charter of Rights and Freedoms
   Journal of Catholic Legal Studies (St. John's School of Law, New York) Symposium Issue Vol. 47, 1, 69–96.

9. Donlevy, J.K. (2009). Catholic High School Administrators and the Inclusion of Non-Catholic Students
   Journal of Educational Administration [Australia] Vol. 47 No. 5.

10. Donlevy, J.K. (2008). Non-Catholic Students in Catholic High Schools: Two Qualitative Studies
    Journal of Religious Education [Australia] 56 (4) pp. 29–39.

INTRODUCTION

THE FOUNDATIONS

This Introduction looks at inclusion from the position of the Catholic Church as stated in Vatican documents, as viewed by academic researchers, and through the statements of some Catholic organizations. Lastly, it provides an explanation of the methodology and methods I used in researching inclusion in the Canadian provinces of Saskatchewan and Alberta.

THE CATHOLIC CHURCH AND INCLUSION

The Church Fathers of Vatican II gave the invitation to non-Catholics, Christian and non-Christian alike, to send their children to Catholic schools. In *Gravissium Educationis* (Vatican II, 1965b) the Church stated,

> the Church considers very dear to her heart those Catholic schools . . . which are attended also by students who are not Catholics . . . This Sacred Council of the Church earnestly entreats pastors and all the faithful to spare no sacrifice in helping Catholic schools fulfill this function . . . especially in caring for the needs of those . . . who are strangers to the gift of faith (para. 9).

In *Dignitatis Humanae* (Vatican II, 1965a), the Fathers spoke of "the right of man to religious freedom" and that "no one therefore is to be forced to embrace the Christian faith against his own will" and further that "in matters religious every manner of coercion on the part of men should be excluded" (paras. 2 & 9). Indeed, it appears as though the Church had "accepted religious pluralism as integral to human freedom" (McDonald, 2004, p. 209).

The Congregation For Catholic Education (Congregation, 1977) stated in *The Catholic School*, "the Catholic school offers itself to all, non-Christians included, with all its distinctive aims and means, acknowledging, preserving and promoting the spiritual and moral qualities, the social and cultural values, which characterize different civilizations" (para 85).

In 1979, John Paul II in his Apostolic Exhortation, *Catechesi Tradendae* (John Paul II, 1979), spoke of the "ecumenical dimension" of catechetics, which would apply to adults and Catholic school religious instruction, stating that,

> a correct and fair presentation of the other Churches and ecclesial communities that the Spirit of Christ does not refrain from using as means of salvation . . . [as] the Church herself, can exist outside the visible boundaries of the Catholic Church . . . [would in effect] help non-Catholics to have a better knowledge and appreciation of the Catholic Church and her conviction of being the universal help toward salvation (para 32).

In 1982, the same Congregation in *Lay Catholics In Schools: Witnesses To Faith* stated,

> every person has a right to an integral education, an education which responds to all of the needs of the human person (para. 3) . . . [and that] at times there are students in Catholic schools who do not profess the Catholic faith, or perhaps are without any religious faith at all. Faith does not admit of violence; it is a free response of the human person to God as He reveals Himself. Therefore, while Catholic educators will teach doctrine in conformity with their own religious convictions and in accord with the identity of the school, they must at the same time have the greatest respect for those students who are not Catholics. They should be open at all times to authentic dialogue, convinced that in these circumstances the best testimony that they can give of their own faith is a warm and sincere appreciation for anyone who is honestly seeking God according to his or her own conscience (para. 42).

By 1988, however, the Congregation in *The Religious Dimension of Education in a Catholic School* had changed its tone, somewhat, on the topic of inclusion. It reiterated the invitation and that "[t]he religious freedom and the personal conscience of individual students and their families must be respected" but went on to say,

> On the other hand, a Catholic school cannot relinquish its own freedom to proclaim the Gospel and to offer a formation based on the values to be found in a Christian education; this is its right and its duty. To proclaim or to offer is not to impose, however; the latter suggests a moral violence which is strictly forbidden, both by the Gospel and by Church law (para. 6).

The invitation was again extended in 1997 by the Congregation (1997) in *The Catholic School On The Threshold Of The Third Millennium* in saying that, among many other important things, in particular, the institution "is not reserved to Catholics only, but is open to all those who appreciate and share its qualified educational project" (para. 16).

The Catechism of the Catholic Church (Catechism, n.d.) reiterated the above saying that everyone has the right to act in conscience and in freedom so as personally to make moral decisions. It states that "[the individual] . . . must not be forced to act contrary to his [or her] conscience. Nor must he [or she] be prevented from acting according to his [or her] conscience, especially in religious matters" (para. 1782).

To encapsulate, the Catholic Church invites all who sincerely wish to share and participate in the objectives of Catholic education to enter the Catholic school community. The promise is of a Christian based education within a faith community where knowledge of the Catholic faith is taught, lived, and shared with non-Catholics. They are sincerely invited to dialogue with others about their faith and beliefs in an atmosphere of both freedom of conscience and religion. It was through these documents that "the Vatican congregation with jurisdiction over the educational institutions in the Church [had] asserted control over Catholic schools at the pre-university level" (Nuzzi, 2004a, p. 17).

Although Rome had spoken, each country was to interpret the above documents in their implementation. In the United States, reference may be made to four documents, "To Teach as Jesus Did" (United States Conference of Catholic Bishops, 1972), "Teach Them" (National Conference of Catholic Bishops, 1976), "Sharing the Light of Faith" (National Conference of Catholic Bishops, 1979), "Renewing Our Commitment to Catholic Elementary and Secondary Schools in the Third Millennium" (United States Conference of Catholic Bishops, 2005). However, in Canada, the voice of the Canadian Conference of Catholic Bishops has not produced similar guidance.

SCHOLARS AND INCLUSION

There are only a few scholarly treatments in the United States and Canada dealing either directly or indirectly with the inclusion of non-Catholic students in Catholic schools. In general, it is fair to say that non-Catholic parents in the United States rank academic program, teaching of moral and spiritual values, discipline, religious atmosphere, and safety, *in that order*, as the primary reasons they send their children to Catholic school (Hickey, 1983; Penn, 1985). In Canada's publicly supported Catholic schools, where no financial sacrifice is required on the part of parents who send their children to Catholic schools, mere convenience is also a factor for sending their children to Catholic schools (McKay, 2002; Jelinski, 1994).

Seeley (2000) states that being non-Catholic "did not play a significant role in their feelings that they were part of the school community" (p. 84), that "friends were the essential core of the school community for the participants" (p. 82), and that "most of the participants' responses to questions about Catholicism as a formal religion were either negative or neutral" (p. 85).

RESEARCH IN TWO CANADIAN PROVINCES (SASKATCHEWAN & ALBERTA)

My research into inclusion involved, amongst other things, four qualitative studies conducted in two Western Canadian provinces. The first study was concerned with Catholic high school students and Catholic teachers. The second involved six Catholic school administrators. The third was concerned with ten non-Catholic students who had recently graduated from a Catholic high school. The fourth sought understanding from twelve non-Catholic high school students.

All four studies utilized Grounded Theory as a methodology, documentary analysis, and either or both of video-taped focus group research or audio recorded or video-taped personal interviews.

Presented hereafter is a general discussion of the chosen methodology followed by a statement for each of the four studies. The research questions, contexts, procedures, reason for the choice of a particular procedure, and an explanation of the analysis which was used, are provided.

THE METHODOLOGY: GROUNDED THEORY AS ESPOUSED BY GLASER (1992, 1998) AND STRAUSS AND CORBIN (1998)

The methodology I chose for my research into inclusion was objectivist grounded theory. Charmaz (2000) describes grounded theory methodology as being split into two schools: objectivist and constructionist (p. 150).

The objectivist school is divided into two camps, typified by the works of Glaser (1998) and Strauss and Corbin (1998). Both accept that there is a reality independent of the researcher, and thus, Charmaz (2000) designates their methodological schools as proffering an objectivist grounded theory.

Glaser's (1998) position often comes close to traditional positivism, with its assumptions of an objective, external reality, a neutral observer who discovers data, reductionist inquiry of manageable research problems, and objectivist rendering of data. Strauss and Corbin's (1998) stance assumes an objective external reality, aims toward unbiased data collection, proposes a set of technical procedures, and espouses verification (p. 510). Glaser holds that rigidity is inherent in the quantitative paradigm due to its dependence on an *a priori* research question, strict and prescriptive operating procedures, and its stress on validity and verification of the emerging theory and hypothesis. That is why he and his former acolyte, Strauss, developed grounded theory. Thus, he eschews this methodology which he refers to as an entirely new methodology which he calls "full conceptual description" (p. 2). He argues for his version which stresses that the research question emerges from the data *a posteriori* and that there must be great flexibility in the process of researching wherein the researcher receives guidance from the participants. It is this consonance with basic qualitative "flexibility of method" and indeed conceptualizing that leads to the discovery of understandings and beliefs within the context of the participants' life world. He holds this to be of utmost importance for both research and to the development of theory. He further argues that to focus on process methodology rather than the development of theory from the data is wrong-headed and in fact not "true" grounded theory (p. 6). In effect, it is suggested that his position is reminiscent of the advice to the caterpillar that it ought not to focus on its number of legs or how they move in sequence but on the experience of walking. Glaser (1998) holds that this focus on procedures and method forces data into categories. This "forcing is a normative projection, a learned preconception, a paradigmatic projection, a cultural organization . . . As the intolerance of confusion increases so does forcing" (pp. 81-82). His contention is that "all is data" is lost when one focuses upon the process of coding and creating categories,

> In prematurely focusing on a theoretical code, such as pacing, or a unit, the researcher becomes lost in description instead of generation of theory with theoretical completeness . . . Focusing only on one unit fosters (1) the quantitative canons of evidentiary research linked with time and place, such as verification, not generation, and (2) making a false distinction between quantitative and qualitative research. (p. 85)

The research field methodology employed in all four of the studies by this author was Grounded Theory as espoused by Glaser (1992, 1998).

THE FOUR STUDIES

Study #1: Researching Catholic Students, Catholic Teachers, and Inclusion

The first study was conducted in 2001-2002 as I was pursuing a doctorate in educational administration at the University of Saskatchewan. I sought to research inclusion in four urban Catholic high schools in that province, involving four points of investigation: the documents of the Church, academic papers, readings from various non-academic authors, and focus group research in those schools.

The Research Questions

- What are the real life experiences of Catholic students and teachers in their relationships with non-Catholic students in Catholic schools?
- Moreover, what, if any, meanings do those Catholic students and teachers attach to their experiences in terms of the sense of their own faith both personally and within the Catholic school faith community?

The context of the participating schools. The doctoral study dealt with the collection of both visual, audio, and through transcription, written data derived from focus group meetings. Each of four Catholic High Schools in Saskatoon, Saskatchewan were represented with ten students from each of Grades 10, 11, and 12. These students were purposefully selected and balanced between the genders in each focus group (see Table 1). Each school also provided one focus group pool of ten Catholic teachers, again, purposefully selected as volunteers by the Christian Ethics teachers from their respective schools.

Table 1. Number and Gender of Participants from Each School

School	Grade 10	Grade 11	Grade 12	Teachers
A	8 (4m, 4f)	8 (4m, 4f)	9 (5m, 4f)	8 (4m, 4f)
B	6 (3m, 3f)	5 (4m, 1f)	5(2m, 3f)	7 (2m, 5f)
C	8 (2m, 6f)	8 (2m, 6f)	8(3m, 5f)	4 (3m, 1f)
D	2 (1m, 1f)	3 (2m, 1f)	5 (4m, 1f)	3 (2m, 1f)

The procedure. The focus group meetings were video-taped and lasted up to two hours in length. Thereafter, they were transcribed for both audio and visual cues.

The focus group questions were derived from the idea that the Catholic school is a place where values are crucial as they are derived from faith and where they are "communicated through the interpersonal and sincere relationships of its members" (Congregation, 1977, para. 32). In particular, questions aimed collectively at revealing Foster's (1982) "spontaneous moments of community" through the experiences of Catholic and non-Catholic students in relationship. For the purposes of this study, there appeared to be no better research tool to peal off the complex layers of meaning which comprised mixtures of faith and other understandings which underlie the participants' individual experiences. Indeed, the communal aspect of the focus group seemed ideally suited to address this study's research questions. The following comments on focus group research bear out that conclusion.

Why choose focus group research?. In this first study on inclusion, which involved my doctoral dissertation, I noted that the Congregation for Catholic Education (1988) states, "What makes the Catholic school distinctive is its attempt to generate a community climate in the school that is permeated by the Gospel spirit of freedom and love" (para. 1). With that statement in mind, it seemed consistent to seek the expression of Catholic students' and teachers' experiences within a group. In other words, it seemed intuitively correct to seek the experiences and meanings of Catholic students and teachers within a group setting. Isolated interviews might have produced individual experiences and meanings. However, those same experiences and meanings, when expressed in a group setting, could reasonably be expected to spark the memories of others in recalling their experiences and how they viewed them. Therefore, focus group research became the chosen method for the first study which was the foundation for my doctoral work.

Beck, Trombetta, and Share (1986) provided an operative definition of focus group research as, "an informal discussion among selected individuals about specific topics relevant to the situation at hand" (p. 73). The process has an overriding assumption that when correct procedures in sampling and process are completed, individuals will express their ideas, beliefs, feelings, attitudes, and understandings of the phenomenon under discussion. It is in the plurality of interaction that focus groups have their greatest benefit to the researcher as this dynamic process reveals the subjective understandings of the individual in dynamic relationship with the group. The perceived experiences and their meanings to both the individual and the group, inter-relating in dynamic relationship, reveals the commonalities of opinion which is clearly within the qualitative paradigm. Vaughn (1996) suggests that it is this which best reflects the phenomenological nature of social reality (p. 16). However, the process of interpretation of participants' perceptions and the framing of questions by the researcher raises the issue of unwitting bias in leading or moderating the focus group.

Qualitative research warns of the dangers of researcher bias resulting from a conscious or unconscious acceptance of *a priori* assumptions. These assumptions frame questions with implicit answers and blur the interpretation of data. Yet, in focus group research, the moderator has little control over activity generated because the participants interact among themselves, posing questions, responding, clarifying, and even changing positions. In other words, focus groups have a life of their own which reduces the presence, and thus the potential for contamination, of the researcher. The group's cohesiveness in purpose and ostensible, if not actual, philosophical homogeneity produces a self-validating empowerment of the individual, encouraging him or her to voice personal opinions, feelings, and understandings of the issue without the anxiety of being right or wrong vis-à-vis an authority figure. This self-disclosure within a community of disclosure provides a safe environment for participants to explore not only their own but also other participants' feelings, beliefs, perceptions, and understandings in a non-threatening manner.

Vaughn (1996) suggests that there are five good reasons to use focus groups: synergism, snowballing, stimulation, security, and spontaneity. Synergism is created as the group dynamic produces more quality data then individual interviews. Snowballing develops as participants who express their opinions set off chain reactions of dialogue among other participants. Stimulation is generated as comments invite agreement or disagreement from others. Security is created as the participants have been purposely selected with homogeneity in mind to ensure security and foster disclosure. Spontaneity is produced as participants are free to speak when and how they want without any pressure to respond "in order" or in a certain manner (p. 14). These five reasons, along with a few open-ended questions from the researcher, set the stage for focus groups to uncover participants' perceptions.

I should note that a survey method was considered in this study to methodologically triangulate possible findings, but as Morgan (1997) says, "The key defining feature of self-contained focus groups is . . . not the absence of other methods but rather the ability to report data from the focus groups as a sufficient body of knowledge" (p. 21). He says as well that, "the distinguishing feature of a self-contained focus group is that the results of the research can stand on their own" (p. 18). It is true that focus group research can be used to supplement other sources and to be part of a multi-method study, but in this study, the purpose was to explore the unexplored. The singularity of a self-contained focus group study seemed appropriate.

In sum, using focus groups fitted the qualitative research paradigm, the research into inclusion, and provided the benefits of synergism, stimulation, security, and spontaneity to this first study.

Analysis of the focus group data. Once having completed the video-taping, each tape was viewed twice before any writing. Thereafter, the video recordings were transcribed by the researcher, stopping and starting the tapes to grasp what was being said, how it was being said, noting the facial expressions and body language of the participants, and making marginal editorial comments as the process progressed. Words and gestures of the participants were noted in an attempt to understand what was being said not only verbally but also emotively by the participants. Choosing particularly significant moments and text, the researcher focused upon the following questions. Were the expressions repeated frequently by the participants? Were the usages of expressions consistent or were multiple meanings expressed? Were expressions spoken of with emotional intensity and if so, was it consistent with appropriate body language and text? Which ideas were expressed articulately? Were some ideas avoided by the participants: evidenced by their demeanor? Was agreement or disagreement visually evident amongst the participants when a single participant expressed an idea? The above questions represented the criteria for determining the meaningful and significant events in the video-taped sessions.

Following the above process, a professional transcriber was retained to type out the audio portion of the video tapes. Thereafter the texts of those transcripts were compared with the researcher's earlier notes. It was clear that the transcriber's text alone would not have been sufficient to gain an understanding of the participants' ideas in the focus group sessions. The visual cues expressed by non-verbal participants in response to verbal participants' ideas, at times during the sessions, were very valuable in discerning the group's understandings. The initial analysis of the data by the researcher and further analysis using the transcriber's text represented the micro-analysis stage of the analysis.

Following the above analysis, simple tentative categories of participants' ideas were created which related significant and meaningful ideas expressed in the transcripts for which the visual data provided concurrence. Negative concurrence was noted. This axial coding took into account the contingencies of time and space as well as continua along which a word was used and produced a "thickness" to those categories.

Selective coding followed the above, which related the categories to each other: i.e., Category "A" Community, Category "B" Faith, "Unified Category" Faith Community. A further review of the video tapes provided depth of data to those categories after which followed a linking of the various unified categories into broader concepts which in turn were inter-related where it appeared to be reasonable to do so. Samples of the process using actual text from the focus group sessions were provided in the final document (Donlevy, 2003a).

It was from the above analytical process, as well as data from other sources as stated hereafter, that ten major categories emerged in relation to inclusion. Other matters were evident in the data, but none had the same significance or clarity as the ten dimensions.

The study, from which the title of this book was derived, was not seeking to discover or examine the various dimensions of inclusion. Rather, it sought to understand the participant Catholic teachers' and Catholic students' experiences with inclusion. With that objective in mind it was expected that pedagogical, social, psychological, spiritual, and philosophical themes would emerge from the focus group sessions. However, secondary themes dealing with race, culture, politics, finance, and the law, fortuitously become apparent from data supplied by central office administrators, school principals, various pieces of correspondence from third party sources, as well as a reading of the enabling educational statute. These secondary themes, although ostensibly tangential to the basic study, were clearly of great importance to a broader understanding of the phenomenon.

This first study was the foundational piece for all my future research into inclusion and its findings are referred to throughout this book.

Study #2: Catholic School Administrators and Inclusion

The second study involved an exploration of the administrative aspects of inclusion with consideration of the available relevant school board policies and through telephone interviews with six Catholic high school principals.

The Research Questions

- What Catholic school board and Catholic high school policies are in place which govern the admission of non-Catholic students?
- In the opinion of the participating Catholic high school principals, what are the stated objectives and reasons for those policies?
- In the opinion of the participating Catholic high school principals, do those policies achieve their objectives?
- In the opinion of the participating Catholic high school principals what might be changed or amended in those policies to better achieve the objectives?

Context of the schools. This study involved six urban schools from one school division in a Western Canadian province. The school district stretches over a very wide area incorporating several small urban communities, with thirteen schools, but only six schools have students from Grades 7 to 12 (see Table 2). The six Catholic school principals from those six schools made up the pool of participants for this study.

Table 2. Relevant Data from Each School in the Study

School*	Number of Grade 7-12 students	Percentage of non-Catholic students**	Race in Grades 7-12	Rural & Urban	Socio-Economic Status
A	673	15%	Caucasian	Urban	Upper-Middle
B***	295	32%	All Caucasian except 5	Urban	Upper-Middle
C	130	15-20%	Caucasian	Mixed	
D	81	31%	Caucasian	Rural	Middle to Middle-Lower
E	438	35-40%	All Caucasian except 6	Mixed	Middle to Middle-Lower
F	300	33%	Caucasian	Urban	Middle

* Only one school principal in this study was female.

** Almost all non-Catholic students were noted as being Caucasian and Christian: Lutheran, United Church, and Pentecostal.

***In School B, the official school records indicate that the Catholic student population is 80% but self-identification as Catholic by students in this school resulted in that percentage dropping to 58% of the student body.

The religion program in that district is The Canadian Catechetical Series "We are Strong Together" produced by the Canadian Conference of Catholic Bishops (n.d.) as the principal resource for Grades 7 to 9. At the 10, 11, and 12 grade levels, three locally developed courses are employed which were approved by the relevant Canadian province: Moral Decision Making, Justice, and Peace; A History of the

Catholic Church and Comparative Study of Religion; and Vocational Lifestyle Choices.

Documentary analysis. The pertinent school board regulation (Appendix A) states the importance of "the concept of ecumenism" and that the school district appreciates "the giftedness of other religious experiences." Further, it is the school principal that makes the decision regarding admission of a non-Catholic student in consideration of the available space, program suitability to the student, special facilities availability if required by the student, and the student and parents' respect and acceptance of the Catholic nature of the school. As part of that process the principal utilizes an interview sheet, which may be adapted by each principal, during the interview with the non-Catholic parents and their children at the time of the initial interview for admission (Appendix B).

Procedure (Method). As earlier stated, this research involved tape-recorded telephone interviews of each of the six participants which were guided in part by a series of questions (Appendix C). Each conversation lasted approximately one hour and was transcribed. Once having completed the telephone interviews, each audio-tape was listened to twice by the researcher before any writing. Thereafter notes on each interview were made by the researcher.

Why choose telephone interviews? Telephone interviews were chosen as the Catholic high schools in this study were in different geographical areas of the relevant province. Due to time limitations this research had to be completed in the winter. Many hours would have been required to drive to and from each school when temperatures would plummet to 30 to 40 degrees below zero Fahrenheit making driving conditions at times dangerous. Although I would have preferred face-to-face conversations in order to assess body language and to get a sense of the school's surroundings and atmosphere, limitations such as distance, weather, cost, and time made, in my opinion, this type of research reasonably acceptable.

Analysis of the data. The telephone interviews focused me on the voice intonation of the participants in an attempt to understand what was being said not only verbally but also emotively. Choosing particularly significant moments in the recorded interview and text, I focused on the following questions: Were the expressions repeated frequently by the participants? Were the usages of expressions consistent or were multiple meanings expressed? Were expressions spoken of with emotional intensity and if so, was it consistent with the text? Which ideas were expressed articulately? Were some ideas avoided by the participants: evidenced by their reluctance to respond? Was agreement or disagreement evident amongst the participants' audio recordings? These questions represented the criteria for determining the meaningful and significant events in the audio-taped interviews.

Thereafter, the texts of the transcripts were compared with my earlier notes. It was clear that the transcriber's text alone would not have been sufficient to gain an understanding of the participants' ideas in the interviews. My initial analysis of the data and further analysis using the transcriber's text represented the micro-analysis stage of the analysis. Following the above analysis simple tentative categories of participants' ideas were created which related significant and meaningful ideas expressed in the transcripts. As in Study #1, negative concurrence was noted and the axial coding took into account the contingencies of time and space as well as continua along which a word was used and produced a "thickness" to those categories. Selective coding followed the above, which related the categories to each another.

It was from the above analytical process that four major themes emerged in relation to inclusion. Other matters were evident in the data but none had the same significance or clarity as the four themes: Theme A: the school administrators' expectations, Theme B: the significance of the preliminary interview, Theme C: the ongoing relationship of the non-Catholic parent and child to the Catholic school community, Theme D: points of confrontation with the Catholic school administration. Thereafter, those themes were reflected upon by the researcher with consideration given to the documents of the Catholic Church and the work of previous researchers.

The details of the findings from this study have been incorporated into the various dimensions of this book.

Study #3: Non-Catholic Student Graduates from a Catholic High School

This third study involved seeking out former non-Catholic students from one of the Catholic high schools in Saskatchewan which had been involved with Study #1. Ten former non-Catholic students comprised the pool of participants. The first non-Catholic student, who had been approached by me, found the other nine participants from those of his acquaintance who had attended the same high school.

The Research Questions

- Is the religion or faith of the non-Catholic student affected by attending a Catholic high school?
- Does the non-Catholic student experience a sense of being the Other within the Catholic high school community?
- Does the non-Catholic student experience the school community as a faith community?
- How do the actions of the Catholic high school teacher affect the perception of the non-Catholic student to the Catholic faith?
- What is of the greatest significance to non-Catholic students in the Catholic high school?

Context. At the time of the students' attendance at their high school, it was the youngest of the city of Saskatoon, one of Saskatchewan's four mainline Catholic high schools. It was opened in 1995. The student population was approximately 900. The students in this study estimated the number of non-Catholics in the school at approximately fifty percent.

There is no data available from the city on this school. However, it should be noted that there is no public high school in that area which caused many teachers to suggest to me that the number of non-Catholic students is quite high due to convenience of attendance. The best information available is from a school administrator who related that although the school draws from a number of areas, it was fair to suggest that the school's student population was from an upper-middle socio-economic area.

While visiting the school on several occasions over several years, as my children attended that school, I have only seen two Afro-Canadian students. Anecdotal evidence from one of the school administrators indicates there are approximately twenty to twenty-five First Nations students and twenty-five international students which includes Asian, Mexican, and South American students in attendance. Interestingly, the Student Representative Council Male President was a non-Catholic (Evangelical) student. The general feeling I had over the years while visiting the school, was that it was a very business-like place where rules and kids were of great importance.

All ten students in this study were Caucasian: eight males and two females. None were married although two were engaged. All had attended the school, and Christian Ethics classes through grades nine to twelve inclusive, graduating from 2004 through 2006. The school used the Grade 9, "We Are Strong Together" series (Canadian Conference of Catholic Bishops, n.d.) while Grades 10, 11, and 12 used three themes, respectively, the Christian Story, Community Called Church, and Christian Lifestyles. No particular texts were used in those courses although a religious coordinator for the school district provided guidance on topic and materials. The religious background of the students follows.

The participants in this study come from eclectic religious backgrounds: Mennonite, Lutheran, Evangelical, agnostic, and atheistic. Although the number of participants is small it seems reasonable to categorize their families based upon the data: Category A, committed Christian families; Category B, non-committed Christian families, Category C, non-religious families. It would have been helpful to have had a fourth category of participants, committed non-Christian families (i.e., Islamic families), but unfortunately no such student participants were available for this study.

Students who came from committed Christian families, Category A, had all attended at least some years of Catholic elementary school before entering the Catholic high school. They felt comfortable using the sign of the cross and the language used at school liturgies, at school Mass, and in Christian Ethic's classes. As one student said "We know the lingo." Their families had oriented them towards an acceptance and respect for matters of faith and hence they felt comfortable when those issues were raised in the school. There were positive reasons for their attending Catholic high school: continuity with elementary school friends, a level of comfort with knowing what to expect in terms of a religious atmosphere, and support from their parents in that decision.

Category B students came from families which were nominally Christian where matters of religion and faith were not normally discussed in their homes and hence the students saw religion and faith as having importance – at best – on the periphery of their lives only at times of crisis or celebration. Although several students had attended a Catholic elementary school, they professed little sense of religion or faith other than at a superficial level. Their parents, as related by the participants, motivating force in sending their children to the Catholic high school was its proximity to their homes.

Category C students' families, as related by the participants, were indifferent to matters of faith and religion as were their children who attended the Catholic high school. These students were a mix of those who had attended a Catholic elementary school and those who had not. Their choice to attend a Catholic high school resulted from merely the closeness of the school to their homes.

These emergent categories became important in the interpretation of the data and the themes and have been incorporated into the various dimensions of this book.

Procedure (Method). This research involved tape-recorded telephone interviews of each of the ten participants which were guided in part by a series of questions (Appendix D) which, as aforesaid, were closely aligned to those used by the researcher four years earlier during interviews with Catholic students at the same school. Each conversation lasted approximately one hour and was transcribed. Thereafter, transcripts of the conversations were mailed to each participant for their perusal and further commentary. Concurrent with the above, once having completed the telephone interviews, each audio-tape was heard twice before any writing. Thereafter, notes on each interview were made by the researcher.

Why choose telephone interviews. My original intention was to fly to the city of Saskatoon in the province of Saskatchewan to interview each student face-to-face. I did attend in that city for that purpose but was unable to arrange the necessary interviews. I was a bit naive to think that former students, each now with very active adult lives, would be necessarily available to be interviewed merely because a researcher had traveled to their city. Although I was able to have a face-to-face interview with one participant, the other nine participants were not available and I returned to my home city of Calgary, Alberta and arranged telephone interviews with them.

Analysis of the data. The procedure for the analysis of the data for the telephone interviews was exactly the same as was employed for Study #2.

Study #4: Non-Catholic Students' Attending Six Catholic High Schools

This study was intended as a major companion piece to my dissertation study which involved a large number of Catholic high school students. It was planned that non-Catholic students within six Catholic schools in Alberta which housed Grades 9 to 12 students would be interviewed in focus groups as was the case with Catholic students in the province of Saskatchewan. This seemed a promising research study as the Catholic school district which agreed to participate had a high number of non-Catholic students and both the Catholic school board and Chief Superintendent were supportive of the study.

Research Questions

(Identical to Study #3)

- Is the religion or faith of the non-Catholic student affected by attending a Catholic high school?
- Does the non-Catholic student experience a sense of being the Other within the Catholic high school community?
- Does the non-Catholic student experience the school community as a faith community?
- How do the actions of the Catholic high school teacher affect the perception of the non-Catholic student to the Catholic faith?

Context. This study involved six Catholic schools with students in Grades 9 to 12. Participants came from all but one of those schools. The administrators in the participating schools qualified their schools as serving an upper middle to lower middle (in one case) class. Four of the five schools were considered to serve an urban population while one served a mixed urban/rural population.

The total number of non-Catholic students in the six Catholic high schools within the school district was 233. Twelve students chose to participate. The total number of non-Catholic parents who could have chosen to participate in the fifth study was approximately 466. Twelve parents chose to participate. I first arranged focus group sessions after school hours and when it became apparent that this would not induce students to attend, I arranged for luncheon focus group sessions with food provided. Nevertheless, the overall student participation rate for the six high schools remained at one half of one percent. It was suggested by some of the Catholic school administrators in the participating schools that non-Catholic parents would be very cautious about having their children participate in any study which singled them out for their opinion on Catholic schools. The implication was that the non-Catholic families must feel vulnerable to school authorities or the Catholic community for any misunderstandings which might occur with possible comments made to a researcher. As one administrator stated "Those families would not want to disturb their children's education." Another school administrator suggested that the low participation rate might be due to the general apathy of high school students. However, given the rate of participation by Catholic students in another research project, that argument seems weak. It should be mentioned that the schools' administrative teams seemed to be in support of this research and indeed, in two cases the administration went to great lengths to stimulate student participation – to no avail.

The result of the above highlights the difficulty in researching the issue of non-Catholic students in Catholic schools at least in so far as such research has been attempted in Alberta and Saskatchewan. Anecdotal evidence suggests that at least some Catholic school districts are not overly supportive of such research as it does involve acknowledging the Otherness of the non-Catholic students in the school system and selecting them out of the student population when what is sought is inclusion within the school's faith community. Moreover, it may well be that as earlier suggested, non-Catholic parents feel that if things are going well there is little reason to potentially jeopardize their children's position as a guest within that faith community – even though such risk was carefully reduced to zero by the researcher.

Procedure (Methods). The method chosen for this research project was focus group research. However, due to the low response and participation rate, only one school lent itself to that method. One interview was face-to-face and video recorded for later analysis. The remainder of the interviews were conducted by telephone and recorded for later transcription.

Analysis of the data. In the case of the video taped focus group session, the analysis followed the pattern for Study #1. At the time of the writing of this book the data gathering and analysis continues, but relevant findings have been incorporated into the book where appropriate.

SUMMARY OF INTRODUCTION

There is every reason to believe that Catholic schools will continue to invite and welcome non-Catholic students into Catholic schools. Indeed, as earlier noted, the welcoming of non-Catholic students is *de rigueur* according to Vatican documents. Moreover, the evidence suggests that many non-Catholic parents see benefits in their children attending Catholic schools and hence the applications for entrance will likely continue at least in the jurisdictions earlier canvassed. Given the phenomenon of the inclusion of non-Catholic students in Catholic schools, I have suggested that research into it would be of value to Catholic schools and, as we shall see later in Chapter One, the societies experiencing this phenomenon. It is to the socio-cultural dimension of inclusion that I now turn.

CHAPTER ONE

THE FIRST DIMENSION OF INCLUSION: SOCIAL/CULTURAL

CULTURE

The social/cultural dimension of inclusion contains many elements. Culturally, non-Catholic students enter the Catholic school community often without having been acculturated into the rituals, symbols, and practices of the faith. The Catholic school seeks to evangelize Catholic students through faith witness and instruction, and hence to generate the love of God, faith, and all others in their lives all within a Catholic faith community. However, that is not the intention of the institution or the school community with regard to non-Catholic students. The non-Catholic student is to be welcomed and cherished as a member of the school community with respect given for her or her religious beliefs and is not to be discriminated against for such beliefs – all the while respecting the student's freedom of conscience. Institutionally, the Catholic school requires from the non-Catholic student respect for the denominational norms within the school and adherence to school policies.

Beyond the above, the non-Catholic student's previous peer culture might have been quite distinct from that of the Catholic school, or at least its espoused behavioral expectations. Further, related to the fifth dimension of race, the non-Catholic student's cultural norms may differ widely from the other students in the school in dress, diet, norms in personal relationships, and the student's understanding of authority and her or his relationship with institutional power structures. It is due to the above matters that inclusion may have a distinct cultural dimension which ought to be recognized by a prudent school administrator.

This administrative sensitivity was noted in one Catholic high school, in Study #1, with a significant number of Muslim students as the administrator stated, "We try to be sensitive to their [Islamic students'] religion's holidays and to the fact that their dress is not in line with how the other kids dress. We point out in the classes that variety is acceptable and to be honored" (Donlevy, 2003a). Nuzzi's (2004b) words, although spoken in the American context, ring true for Canadian Catholic schools,

> every aspect of society is being touched in some way by the increasing cultural diversity of the . . . population, multicultural sensitivity will be a special challenge for religious educators in the beginning of the third millennium of Christianity. (p. 78)

The phenomenon of inclusion of non-Catholic students in Catholic schools arguably also has a wide social significance. It is to that issue that I now turn.

SOCIAL

The Social dimension of inclusion, for the purposes of this book, centers upon that phenomenon and its connection to the common good. In particular, how the phenomenon of inclusion provides an example to the wider society of how – whether through a communitarian or liberal lens – the common good can be served in a pluralistic society. With the above in mind, this Chapter continues with an explanation of the history of the term, the common good, followed by an explanation of the modern conceptual approaches to that term in liberalism and communitarianism, ending with the relevance of inclusion to the same (Donlevy, 2008b).

The History of the Concept

The idea of the common good is not new but its meaning has varied throughout time. The ancients offered the idea that the common good resulted from a cultivation of the virtues and a legislatively good political order in the furtherance of the polis (Aristotle, 350 B.C.E) and that the individual owed service to the state which was not associated with mere self-aggrandizement (Cicero, 1913; Miller, 1996). Aquinas (1948) offered that "since all contraries agree in something common, it is necessary to search for the one common cause for them above their own contrary proper causes (I 49, 3; cf. I 2, 3; II-II, q. 58, 7 ad 2; Keys, 2006).

In later years, the rationale for the common good was formulated as the giving-up of freedoms one might have in a hypothetical state of nature in order to avoid the "nasty, brutish, and short" life of an animal in the wild (Hobbes, 1651). Later, the concept was articulated as the greatest good for the greatest number (Bentham, 1996; Mill, 1975) or as minimal state interference on the individual's freedom of action enabling the operation of the "invisible hand" for the betterment of society (Smith, 1904), or the fostering of individual autonomy free from the strictures of an oppressive society (Rousseau, 1980).

In the modern word, the definition of the common good is divided between two competing views: liberalism and communitarianism. Some might argue that the modern debate is, or ought to be, an ontological rather than a procedural debate (Taylor, 1989), but a debate it certainly has become.

The Modern Discussion

Liberalism and the common good. How can a pluralist democracy in a globalized world achieve – if not social accord – at least the social toleration of differences? Surely, some might say, the twentieth century with its sacrifice of individual rights in the name of the Volk, or the dictatorship of the proletariat, or the best interests of the collective have shown that "the concept of a common good, valid for all mankind, rests on a cardinal mistake" (Berlin, 1959, p. 43).

In response, Liberalism offers a refined definition of the common good as various shades of individual autonomy, universal freedoms and rights (Dworkin, 1985), and value self-determination, (Nozick, 1974) with its focus upon the means to freedom rather than the ends of freedom (Rawls, 1971). It is "[the] result of a process of combining preferences, all of which are counted equally (if consistent with the principles of justice)" (Kymlicka, 2002, p. 220; Rawls, 1988). Liberal neutrality, in terms of the state, "is simply the idea that there is no public ranking of the values of different (justice-respecting) ways of life" (Kymlicka, 2002, p. 218). However, while one strain of liberalism suggests that the state should remain neutral in the matter of an individual's life choices (Ackernam, 1990), another offers that certain values such as rational deliberation, civility, racial and gender equity, equal opportunity, and justice as fairness are settled issues not open for discussion (Gutmann & Thompson, 1990). Indeed, the determination of such societal-wide values in a liberal state has been suggested by some liberals as best determined by a collective interpretation (Sullivan, 1990). Thus Liberalism attempts to define the common good in terms of the individual while acknowledging the social nature of being human.

Justification of this approach is offered by Rawls (1971) through his hypothetical Original Position thus warranting the framing of basic societal rules of fairness and a societal conception of the "right" which ensures universally accepted rights protecting individual freedom in a liberal society. If discord is evident one seeks an "overlapping consensus" (Dworkin, 1987) on at least some basic rights which, by consensus can produce fundamental agreement in a democratic society. If no consensus is possible Richardson (1990) suggests that a political accommodation – a *modus Vivendi* – may be possible among divergent communities within a society for reasons of practical accommodation. Whether or not the issue of value incommensurability amongst communities can be adequately addressed by the above is open to question. Indeed, perhaps Berlin (2002) is correct in saying that this conundrum is never to be totally resolved as it is the tension between the autonomous individual and social pluralism which is inherent to a free democracy. It is certainly true that those who are marginalized, especially historically, within a society will likely require recognition both politically and legally (Wolf, 1992).

In sum, liberalism offers that "the self is prior to the ends which are affirmed by it" (Rawls, 1971, p. 560) and posits the necessity of freedom of choice for those ends in order to develop the autonomous individual. It is the neutrality of the State upon such individually chosen ends that allows for the individual's self determination and indeed the right to revise one's choices. As Kymlicka (2002) states,

> What is central to the liberal view is not that we can perceive a self prior to its ends, but that we understand ourselves to be prior to our own ends in the sense that no end or goal is exempt from possible re-examination. (p. 225)

As such, the individual can detach one's self from communal values and exercise individual judgment – the primary pursuit being not the exercise of that freedom but the particularity of the value chosen.

There is another school of political thought which offers an alternative to the liberal concept of the common good: communitarianism.

COMMUNITARIANISM AND THE COMMON GOOD

"The common good is conceived of [by communitarianism] as a substantive conception of the good life which defines the community's 'way of life'" (Kymlicka, 2002, p. 220). It is a theory which offers that society exists prior to the individual and that it creates the individual's social self. Indeed, because society pre-exists the individual, it provides continuity of the life-world, allowing individuals a place and time within which to function and exercise their capacities through interaction with others, resulting in interdependence. From this interdependence flows the "primordial sources of obligation and responsibility" (Selznick, 1986, p. 5). To be sure, the "me" exists as a separate entity from the collective, but the other part of the person, the "I," exists as the agent of "reflective morality" (p. 3). In that sense, it moves beyond the "individual endorsement" of liberalism (Dworkin, 1987, pp. 16–17) as the communitarian self seeks "social confirmation" (Kymlicka, 2002, p. 278). In what seems in contradiction to liberalism, communitarianism holds that we "all approach our circumstances as bearers of a particular social identity . . . Hence what is good for me has to be the good for one who inhabits these roles" (MacIntyre, 1981, pp. 204–205; Kymlicka, 2002, p. 220). It is this sense of morality, or of what is good, held as a community value which transforms a community from a mere association or grouping of individuals from *Gesellschaft* to *Gemeinschaft* (Tonnies, 1955). It is the community's values, the individual's social context, which set the authoritative horizon which in turn set the parameters of the individual's goals (Taylor, 1979, 157-159; Sandel, 1982, p. 183). The "thin social order" of liberalism gives way to the reality of the "thick social order" of the encumbered self which does not preclude that there is a process of transformation upon rational reflection and hence changing one's goals, between the socially constituted self and the I (Sandel, 1982, p. 183).

It is this "feeling of commitment to a common public philosophy . . . [which] is a precondition to [a] free culture" (Kymlicka, 1990, pp. 122–123). Those in the community have a responsibility to defend the common values when under attack by others from within because failing to do so would result in the "debasement and decay" of the community's values and ultimately of the community itself (Dworkin, 1985, p. 230).

In communitarianism, individuals' freedoms and rights are not denied but are circumscribed and flow from the peace, order, and good government of the community with enforcement – at its best – through persuasion and social opprobrium. Such an approach is possible because interrelationships are the grist to action within society. To be an outcast is so restrictive to individuals that they will, theoretically, stop the offending behavior (Etzioni, 1998, p. xii).

Thus, unlike liberalism simpliciter, which posits the primacy of autonomy and individual rights with few social restrictions – the thin social order – communitarianism offers that a necessary precondition to freedom and rights is a society that possesses common values which justify many reasonable restrictions on the individual to protect those values – the thick social order. Bellah (1998) states,

> A good community is one in which there is argument, even conflict, about the meaning of the shared values and goals, and certainly about how they will be actualized in everyday life. Community is not about silent consensus; it is a form of intelligent, reflective life, in which there is indeed consensus, but where the consensus can be challenged and changed – often gradually, sometimes radically – over time. (p. 16)

Communitarianism is about individuals living in community where they maintain their individual free will but where their personage is formed through a common language, values, and concepts that in turn frame reality and cause them to relate to that world and the people in it with the values of the community.

The common good described in the liberal and communitarian traditions are powerful displays of the human intellect as it attempts to resolve issues of great import to democratic societies which due to globalization in its economic, political, and cultural aspects seem at times to be fractured and divided amongst themselves.

Inclusion and the Common Good

Liberalism and inclusion. The inclusion of non-Catholic students into Catholic schools makes a contribution to a conception of the common good as it serves as an exemplar to a democratic society conflicted by the difficulty of embracing the good as expressed in both liberalism and communitarianism.

Catholic schools recognize the crucial significance of the individual's conscience not only through Church documents which ensure the students' right to freedom of conscience and freedom of religion but also in practice (Congregation, 1982, para. 42) . A recent study of non-Catholic students in a Catholic high school (Donlevy, 2008a) found such freedom expressed in that ultimately, although the school provided the opportunity and prompting for an encounter with the religious or spiritual aspects of life, it was up to the student to choose to enter into that encounter. A non-Catholic student said, "I think it's whether you want to take the opportunity of the Catholic high school or not." Another non-Catholic students stated, "I opted not to immerse myself in it" (Study #3); and a third said:

> Catholic high school helped me discover who I was. It helped me – like kind of being all by myself [as a non-Catholic in a classroom] it helped me deepen my strength and it helped me deepen my relationship with Christ and it helped me ask those questions that I'd never asked before but I wanted to ask . . . It really helped me to strengthen my relationship with Christ.

It is the "overlapping consensus" of the values of dignity, equality, fairness, justice, respect for others, which are found in all faiths which provide basic value cohesion for all within a Catholic school. Catholic schools do not seek to evangelize the non-Catholic student but to invite the student to experience the Catholic reality within the school. The non-Catholic student may choose her or his faith and the liberal principal of revisability is honored within the Catholic school. It is a matter of respect for and exercises of the individual's conscience which is sacrosanct.

The Congregation for Catholic Education (1982) stated that the Church has,

> the greatest respect for those students who are not Catholics . . . [and teachers] should be open at all times to authentic dialogue, convinced that in these circumstance the best testimony that they can give of their own faith is a warm and sincere appreciation for anyone who is seeking God according to his or her own conscience (para. 42).

Moreover, the idea of a symbiotic relationship and reciprocity in the meeting of faiths, as opposed to religions, between the Catholic and non-Catholic students was stated by a Grade 12 Catholic student.

> You feed off each other, and if all your feeding [is from the] people . . . who are the same as you, that is good, but it can only offer you so much. But when you have people with different views – different beliefs, it heightens yours and it brings them up at the same time so everyone just grows . . . maybe not in the same direction of growth but you will grow to a better understanding and more mature life (Study #1 as cited in Donlevy 2003a).

In that encounter there is an opportunity for all students to grow spiritually. A Grade 10 Catholic student said,

> Non-Catholic people help me grow my faith not so much that they share views . . . not that I'm going to convert, I'm still Roman Catholic, but they make me view something different in . . . [my] life. [I think] Oh yeah! That would be an interesting way to praise God (Study #1).

A Grade 12 Catholic student related, "It's good to have someone to challenge our faith, and to have someone to help make us stronger" (Study #1).

It is the presence of non-Catholic students and thus the relationships which Catholic students have with their non-Catholic friends in the school which demands that the Catholic student listen and accept the "Other" for who they are as persons and thus live the ideals or beliefs of acceptance, understanding, and respect. To quote one Grade 11 Catholic student, "We need these people [the non-Catholics] to put into practice Jesus' teachings" (Study #1). The above quotations give strength to Seeley's (2000) finding that of the non-Catholic students she interviewed, "none felt excluded for their religious beliefs" (p. 82) and further as Maritain (1962) says, the Catholic school "invites not submission but dialogue and encounter" (p. 54).

The democratic values of respect, fairness, justice, and inclusion, are deepened and separated from the mundane of the day to day life of students and teachers through prayer, liturgies, and Mass in the school. As one Catholic student stated,

> [Mass] puts or tries to put the emphasis on something else [rather than the secular]. I think that it gives people sort of something else to think about besides the normal stuff, bigger and more important than just . . . grades (Study #1).

The above quotations indicate that the Catholic school community through inclusion displays a rejection of sectarianism which is “a bigoted and intolerant exaltation of one’s own group that absolutizes the true and the good of its members, encouraging prejudice against anyone who has [an] alternative identity – especially immediate neighbors” and parochialism which “reflects a narrow-minded, self-sufficient, and insular mentality that closes up within itself, is intolerant to or oblivious of other perspectives, and conceited about its own” (Groome, 1998, pp. 42, 44).

It seems a paradox that for some non-Catholic students the Catholic school is a spiritually liberating experience. Yet, as a non-Catholic student participant stated with respect to prayer, liturgies, and Mass in the school:

> there was a Christian influence there and its something important to me . . . you can talk about [God] without being afraid [of] political incorrectness. . . [of being] offensive to someone else. . . . That’s an issue nowadays . . . what if there is someone in the room who isn’t a Catholic or Christian (Study #3).

Another related how she felt about Morning Prayer in the school,

> the more that you’re exposed to that [the idea of God] the more you’re reminded [of God]. Whether it’s through morning prayer or Mass . . . I think that helps bring you back on to the right path, its a reminder about what’s important (Study #3).

A third non-Catholic student was asked by the researcher, “Did going to a Catholic high school effect your faith?” The student responded, “Yes, definitely. You’re taught in a way that you develop yourself spiritually” (Donlevy, 2008a).

In sum, the liberal values of basic rights and freedoms for individuals, the development of a critical sense and the individual’s autonomy, the revisability of one’s positions, as well as the enhancement of fairness, justice, respect for others, and the dignity of the individual are arguably sought to be fostered in the Catholic school and are exemplified by the inclusion of non-Catholic students within the Catholic school community. Moreover, the idea of an overlapping consensus of values is evident. This is what should be expected in Catholic schools as unlike other legitimate institutions the Catholic school is, as the Catholic Church says, “open to all.”

Beyond liberalism, the Catholic school demonstrates to the wider society its conception of the communitarian common good.

Communitarianism and Inclusion.

The Catholic Church, as with Communitarianism, sees the crucial importance of the experiences of past generations and their legacy of values (Vatican II, 1965a, para. 5). Within the school, the systematic formation of students takes place, and, in that process, students experience the meaning and truth of their personal experiences (Congregation, 1977, para. 27). It is the sharing of the same vision, the same values, and thus the same educational norms within the school community that makes the school Catholic (para. 3). The Catholic school, besides the ordinary pedagogical goals, transmits the values of faith and reason to its students.

The Church holds (Congregation, 1982) that teachers in Catholic schools (para. 6) "bring to life in the students the *communitarian* dimension of the human person . . . [as] every human being is called to live in a community, as a social being, and as a member of the People of God" (para. 22) [italics added]. Within the school community, the norms and values of students in the faith are formed by those who teach and interact with them, including fellow students. This transmission of faith is in concert with the transmission of culture and knowledge as seen through the faith. Thus the Catholic school is of the thick social order and, similar to communitarianism, "Christian faith, in fact, is born and grows inside a *community*"(Congregation, 1977, para. 30) [italics added].

The Catholic school seeks to produce students who have experienced the implicated self and, as Selznick (1986) noted, "The morality of the implicated self builds on the understanding that our deepest and most important obligations flow from identity and relatedness" (p. 7). Further, it is the anchored rationality of communitarianism, solidly fixed in concrete reason that is "in part, the funded experience of the political community" (Selznick, 1986, p. 14). The latter is comparable with the Church's position that truth is not the result of consensus but rather a flow from "a consonance between intellect and objective reality" (John Paul II, 1998, para. 56).

This community is experienced by its members in three ways (Foster, 1982): (a) through rituals and symbols connecting to the community's past that is acknowledged and shared (p. 56); (b) through bonding relationships with "institutional structures, customs, and kinship networks" (pp. 56-57) that guide through trust and mediate people in their relationships with others; and (c) through experiencing a spontaneous moment of egalitarian commonality with others, where "participants are not known to one another by their roles, jobs, or positions, but in the commonality of their submission to the power of the moment" (p. 58). In these spontaneous moments of community, members experience the spaciousness of time, the intimacy of the transcendent, and the transformation of the immediate (p. 58).

The Church's belief is that the crucial communitarian element of the Catholic school is a sense of belonging due to the common experience of history, belief, and purpose experienced in the present. Flowing from that belief, the Catholic school has the task of transmitting to students, by various means, the specific norms, values, and beliefs of the Catholic Faith. That transmission seems to be effective "not so much through formal religious instruction class but rather through the closeness of the Catholic community that the experiences of attending Catholic school generate" (Seeley, 2000, p. 167).

It appears that a communitarian understanding of community permeates the group and is crystallized at least in expression at times of crisis, yet where difference is accepted and allowed to flourish in a respectful social atmosphere. It is this "communal emphasis regarding human and Christian existence" (Groome, 1996, p. 108) evidenced by inclusion which stresses the *virtue of solidarity* (John Paul II, 1988, para. 9) among those in the school community.

The solidarity above is reflected in the democratic value of acceptance of the Other as evidenced in the words of a Grade 10 and the words of a Grade 12 Catholic student.

> If you have non-Catholics [in the school] you can benefit from that because . . . then you wouldn't want to be snobby to them saying they weren't good enough to be around . . . it gives you the opportunity to practice your faith in accepting people (Study #1).

> On our Grade 12 retreat we were there for a couple of days [and] you kinda get to know these [non-Catholic] people . . . . It was really neat how we could all connect. Some people came back really thinking about the faith and not so much letting the Catholic rules getting in the way. Like the more important stuff like seeing God in other people (Study #1).

Nuzzi (2004b) states that "every aspect of society is being touched in some way by the increasing cultural diversity of the . . . population, multicultural sensitivity will be a special challenge for religious educators in the beginning of the third millennium of Christianity" (p. 78).

Catholic teachers may also be deeply affected through inclusion and thus by such acceptance of diversity and plurality within their school as exhibited by the following comment by a Catholic teacher. "When you have a non-Catholic kid, who you know is non-Catholic, come to you and ask you to pray for her family, you know you've done something beyond just Catholicism. There's more to it than just being Catholic" (Study #1).

Bryk, Lee, and Holland (1993) sum up a major aspect of communitarianism within the Catholic school as evidenced by inclusion. They state,

> schooling demands an impassioned rationality shaped by a vision of the common good, a vision that itself is always open to challenge and clarification. Such an education is accomplished through inspiration, not coercion, through dialogue, not dogma. It involves not only classroom teaching but also participation in a communal life that exemplifies its values. (p. 320)

In sum, the communitarian idea of the common good with its concepts of the situated self, the importance of the community's values and history, the importance of relationships, social solidarity, the importance of Gemeinschaft, respect and interaction with the other, and the need for the ethic of care expressed beyond the self, are all evidenced in the Catholic school particularly through its practice of the inclusion of non-Catholic students. As with liberalism, the individual's conscience is of prime importance but for the Catholic school, the person's conscience resides not within the solitude of the individual but rather calls the person to his or her personal interior temple wherein natural law exists and where God resides as counselor (John Paul II, 1993).

One can conclude that as Bryk et al. (1993) state, "we discern nothing fundamentally undemocratic about Catholic school's educational philosophy of person-in-community and their ethical stance of shaping the human conscience toward personal responsibility and social engagement" (p. 341). Moreover, as Langan (1990) states, "Catholicism provides one pattern of what the effort to combine communitarian and liberal values might look like" (p.113).

SUMMATION

In summation, it is fair to say that the cultural/social dimension of inclusion offers society an example of how multiculturalism and diversity may be nurtured and fostered within the Catholic school. That example is an exemplar for the combining of the liberal and communitarian concepts of the common good, exemplified in the Catholic school's policy of the inclusion of children of other faiths. In particular, the liberal concepts of the development of personal autonomy through critical rational thought, freedom of conscience and religion, the principle of revisability, and the crucial importance of teaching the young about fairness, justice, equality, and respect for diversity – as democratic ideals – are evidenced in inclusion. Moreover, the communitarian ideals of the importance of the individual developing within a community's historical context, values, and with an understanding of the importance and responsibility owed to others because of personal conscience was stated. To reiterate, the conclusion reached by this researcher is that inclusion exemplifies the common good both for liberals and communitarian ideals and could, therefore, serve as an exemplar for the wider democratic, pluralistic society.

CHAPTER TWO

THE SECOND DIMENSION OF INCLUSION: POLITICAL

The political aspects of inclusion are complex. The political will of the Catholic laity that have in past generations vigorously defended constitutionally protected Catholic schools may be weakening. In the Canadian provinces of Newfoundland-Labrador and in Quebec, Catholic schools no longer have constitutional protection (Canadian Catholic School Trustees: St John's Convention, 2006; Smith, Foster, & Donahue, 1999) and the constitutionally protected Catholic schools in Ontario, Saskatchewan, and Alberta are under threat.

In Ontario there has been a concerted attack on publicly funded Catholic education from a variety of sources (Canadian Civil Liberties Association, Sept. 24, 2007; Swan, 2007). That attack has been based in part upon a decision by the United Nations Human Rights Committee which found that the funding of Catholic schools by the Ontario Government, while the latter failed to fund other denominations' religious schools, was discriminatory (Canadian Broadcasting Company, November 5, 1999).

In Saskatchewan there appears to be a growing, or at least a persistent, attack on the public funding of Catholic schools. The basic argument appears to be that Catholic schools are divisive and unduly duplicate the costs of public expenditures for education (Morgan, 2001). Moreover, in Alberta it is alleged that publicly funded and constitutionally protected Catholic schools have acted to entice and register non-Catholic students and have thereby deleteriously affected the financial viability of Public schools (Donlevy, 2006a).

A point should be made with respect to the above allegation which has been identified by Mulligan (1999, p. 185). It is one thing to accept those non-Catholics who willingly seek to attend Catholic schools. It is another to poach non-Catholic students to populate a Catholic school. The latter course is politically dangerous for Catholic schools as to do so provides grist to those who would be pleased to see the demise of constitutionally protected publicly funded Catholic school in Ontario, Alberta, and Saskatchewan. This point will be addressed further under the Financial Dimension of inclusion.

Given the above, it appears that the argument for the continued existence of Catholic schools as constitutionally protected and publicly funded institutions in Ontario, Alberta, and Saskatchewan ought best to be strengthened by the argument earlier stated under the First Dimension: the common good. Beyond the constitutional argument, it is helpful to say to the Canadian body politic that Catholic schools benefit all of society, as they contribute to the society's common good because its focus is on the welfare of the community thus making "a potentially unique contribution . . ." to the common good in society (Hollenbach, 1996, p. 100). Indeed, as inclusion serves many religious communities by providing them with a religious, albeit Catholic, alternative to public education, inclusion should have a positive effect on the acceptance of Catholic schools in the public square.

The above argument for Catholic schools and the acceptance of the phenomenon of inclusion seems in concert with the belief that in a multi-cultural democratic mosaic such as Canada, it is to the benefit of the body politic to have a religiously-based constitutionally protected school system to ensure that those of a religious view have a school where a deity is acknowledged. In counterpoint to the argument that such schools should be constitutionally protected, it might be argued that constitutional guarantees are not necessary for such schools to exist. Evidence for that proposition may be such seen in Alberta's Edmonton Public School District as a school of Judaic faith exists in that system. However, such schools exist at the pleasure of the public school board and hence this arrangement does not offer secure protection for future funding.

Politically, constitutionally protected Catholic schools which seek to enroll non-Catholic students run the risk of antagonizing the wider body politic. That is a concern in the public square, but internally Catholic schools face parents of non-Catholic students wanting some say in the education of their children within the Catholic school. In response to such demands, it seems settled law that at least in Ontario, Alberta, and Saskatchewan the parents of non-Catholic students may not sit as Catholic school Trustees. Interestingly, that may not be the case in other Canadian jurisdictions where Catholic schools are not constitutionally protected. A recent case (Yellowknife Catholic Schools v. Euchner, 2007; see also Catholic Civil Rights League, 2007) held both at trial and on appeal that where there is no constitutional protection, a non-Catholic may run as the Catholic school Trustee. That case, which may be appealed, if upheld, would not bode well for Catholic schools where constitutional protection does not exist.

It thus appears that there is a political dimension to inclusion respecting the number of non-Catholic students allowed into Catholic schools. Moreover, on the school level, it is a political question respecting how much input many non-Catholic parents should have in the Catholic school's "parents-advisory" councils. In one case, a diocesan priest attended such a meeting in Saskatchewan to find that none of the elected parent representatives for that school's parent's council were Catholic. Is this a concern? Yes, but the political concern is not that non-Catholic parents are involved in their children's school, but rather that Catholic parents failed to become involved, let alone take a leadership role in the parent-advisory council. Politically, such news made public would have caused scandal in the school district. The diocesan priest quickly appointed Catholic parents to that council.

It seems clear that inclusion has a very active and dynamic political dimension.

CHAPTER THREE

THE THIRD DIMENSION OF INCLUSION: FINANCIAL

The Third dimension of inclusion deals with finance. In the Canaduian Provinces of Saskatchewan, Alberta, and Ontario, Catholic schools are constitutionally protected; therefore, the funding of those schools is required by law. In other Canadian jurisdictions, government funding is at the discretion of the provincial or Territorial governments as their Catholic schools are independent or private faith-based schools, no different than other religious denominations' schools (Wilson, 2007).

In Saskatchewan, school districts have two sources of funding. The first is from the municipal mill rate which is set by the local Public and Separate (Catholic) school boards. In the normal course, a municipality's Public and Catholic school boards act in concert, by way of a "gentlemen's agreement," to ensure that their mill rates are the same in order to prevent municipal rate-payers from choosing to send their children to the least expensive school district.

The second source of funding for each school board comes directly from the Saskatchewan Government in the form of a grant. In 2005, the Provincial Government paid school districts the following sums for each student registered within their jurisdiction: Kindergarten ($2,478), Grades 1 to 5 ($2,478), Grades 6 to 9 ($5,070), and Grades 10 to 12 ($5, 661) (Paslawski, Executive Secretary, Saskatchewan School Trustees' Association: Catholic Section, personal communication, October 12, 2005).

Although the actual cost of educating a student in a school district varies from district to district, it normally costs more per student than the value of the grant. Hence, Catholic school districts which admit non-Catholic students receive the provincial grant, but not that student's parent's municipal tax levy, thereby subsidizing such attendance (Paslawski, Executive Secretary, Saskatchewan School Trustees' Association: Catholic Section, personal communication, October 12, 2005). The public school districts' position is that a portion of the grant for each non-Catholic student attending Catholic schools should be allocated to the public school system, or another source of funds used to compensate the public school system for the loss of the grant.

Beyond the above, once a Catholic school district has admitted non-Catholic students at, for the sake of argument, approximately 30% of the student population, that percentage translates into buildings, supplies, support staff, teachers, and administrators to serve those students (Donlevy, 2006a). Further, all of those requirements coalesce into various vested interests, largely unarticulated, involving teachers, administrators, and the Catholic school bureaucracy itself, to maintain, if not expand, the presence of non-Catholic students in the Catholic school district.

Interestingly, Catholic schools in Saskatchewan may refuse to enroll non-Catholic students up to and including Grade 8, but may not refuse to admit non-Catholic students in Grades 9 to 12.

Alberta's Catholic school districts receive the same funding as public school districts from the provincial government although a record is kept with respect to the number and names of Catholic rate-payers within a Catholic School board's jurisdiction. Interestingly, since the creation of that province in 1905, Catholic schools have received funding for all grades while in the adjacent province of Saskatchewan, which was also created in 1905 from the North West Territories, funding was constitutionally protected only from Grades 1 to 8.

Today in Alberta, Catholic schools receive no extra financial benefit or deficit with the enrollment of non-Catholic students. However, as earlier stated, some in the public school systems argue that when a significant number of non-Catholic students are enrolled in Catholic schools the ability of the public school systems to offer their programs may be deleteriously affected. This is the argument being offered by one public school district in Alberta to the expansion of a Catholic school district's boundaries to geographically include a former public school (Donlevy, 2006a). That matter is currently being litigated in Alberta (Board of Trustees of Aspen View Regional Division No. 19 and Sidney Kuryliw v. Attorney General).

In Ontario, funding for non-Catholic students in Catholic schools follows the same rather complex formulae as for Catholic students. The Catholic school board's budget process involves, in effect, submitting a bill to the Provincial government and in turn receiving payment per pupil. In Ontario, Catholics are electors not rate-payers as there is no other funding for Catholic schools. In one Northern Catholic school district, the amount per Catholic elementary student is approximately \$10,000 and \$11,500 to \$12,000 per Catholic high school student (J. Borst, personal communication, May 27, 2008). In Ontario, Catholic elementary schools may refuse to enroll non-Catholic students, but from Grades 9 to 12 non-Catholic students must be admitted to Catholic high schools.

As mentioned earlier, Mulligan (1999) noted a major concern in his recent research into Canada's Catholic schools. He noted that some Catholic school districts in Canada actually seek to recruit non-Catholic students into Catholic schools. What results is, paradoxically, an economic and bureaucratic dependence on inclusion. This financial dimension of inclusion can affect the formation, or lack thereof, of a district's inclusionary policy. It is ironic that Catholic high schools which were founded for reasons of faith, and for which so much was sacrificed by the originating members of the Catholic community, should now be in a situation where their financial security is defined at least in part by the apparent financial dimension of inclusion.

CHAPTER FOUR

THE FOURTH DIMENSION OF INCLUSION: LEGAL

This Chapter, under Part A, provides the legal basis for the inclusion of non-Catholic students in Catholic schools in the three Canadian provinces of Ontario, Alberta, and Saskatchewan. Part B utilizes a recent legal case (Hall, 2002) and looks at the substantive and procedural rights of a dissentient Catholic student who arguably acted in breach of the norms of the Catholic faith and extends that analysis to hypothetical non-Catholic students in suggesting their legal rights – at least those which may be procedural in nature. Part C is quite long as in order to establish a connection between freedom of conscience as it is juridically understood under the Charter and as the term conscience is understood in the Catholic Church, it is necessary to examine Canadian case law, scholarly works, and official documents of the Catholic Church. Thereafter, that connection is discussed in terms of freedom of conscience within Catholic schools and its significance to the legal rights of dissentient non-Catholic students.

PART A

The Legal Basis for Inclusion

In the three Canadian provinces where inclusion is constitutionally protected, Ontario, Alberta, and Saskatchewan, provincial legislation provides some guidelines for the admission of non-Catholic students.

In Ontario, non-Catholic students do not have a clear right to attend Catholic elementary schools as under section 33(3) a baptismal certificate would normally be required for entrance (Education Act, R.S.O. 1990, C. E.2.).

However, in practice, where there is ample room in a Catholic elementary school and further where non-Catholic parents are willing to sign an agreement that their child or children will attend religious education instruction and participate in all classroom activities, their children will be admitted. Section 35(1) slightly amends this principle as it deals with a pupil's right to attend a more accessible elementary school.

In Ontario's Catholic high schools there is a requirement that non-Catholic students be accepted for admission as that was part of the political and legal quid pro quo for the extension of provincial funding for Catholic high schools in that province.

In Alberta, under the School Act (2000), Catholic schools are not required to accept non-Catholic students but in practice many such students are accepted where there is adequate space in the school (Donlevy, 2008). Sections 13, 44, and

45 of the School Act allow for the admission of non-Catholics to Catholic schools, but only if, in the opinion of the board, there are sufficient resources to do so.

S.13(3)(a) of the *School Act* gives the board discretion to enroll "resident" students if a program offered in the school is suitable in its opinion. "Resident" is explained in s.44 of the Act. Under s.44 (1) a student is a resident of the board of the district or division in which their parents reside. Under s.44 (3) every individual is presumed to be a resident of a public school district or division, but this is qualified by s.44 (4), which states that where a separate school district is established, an individual residing in its boundaries and who is of the same faith (Roman Catholic or Protestant) is deemed to be a resident of the separate school district.

When the above sections are read together, it is evident that in order to be a "resident" of an Alberta separate school district under s.44 one has to be of the same faith as the district. Once one is established as a resident, the board has discretion to admit that person to the school under s.13 (a). S.13 (b) allows for non-residents to be admitted if resources allow for it. Non-residents of a separate school board district would include those who are deemed residents of the public school board, therefore, allowing for non-Catholic public school residents to be admitted to Catholic schools, albeit only if the board finds there are sufficient resources.

Under s.45 (1), the board is required to ensure that all of its resident students are provided with an education program consistent with the requirements of the Act. S.45 (3) allows the board to enroll a resident student of the board or *another* board in the school on the request of a parent if, in the opinion of the board, there are sufficient resources to accommodate that student. This opens the door to non-Catholics being able to attend Catholic separate schools in Alberta.

The above interpretation appears to be supported by Edmonton Catholic Separate School District no. 7 Administrative policy 103 which states that nonresidents of the board (who could be public school board residents, therefore, non-Catholic) may be enrolled provided there are adequate resources available. Adherence to Catholicism is not a requirement, but "All students are expected to participate in the religious life of the school at least to the level of being respectfully attentive."

In Saskatchewan, non-Catholic students may attend a Catholic high school from Grades 9 to 12 (Newton, n.d.), but have no legal right to attend a Catholic elementary school. Section 145 of the Education Act (1995) states:

> Access to high schools
>
> 145(1) Notwithstanding any other provision of this Act, any person who is a resident of a city in which a public school division and a separate school division have been established may declare his or her intention to enroll one or more of his or her children who are eligible to register in Grade 9, 10, 11 or 12 in a school in either the public school division or the separate school division.

(2) A declaration of intention pursuant to subsection (1) is to be given in writing to the boards of education of the school divisions affected prior to June 1 in any year and is effective from the commencement of the next following school year.

(3) Where a declaration of intention is made pursuant to this section, the maker of the declaration is entitled, on behalf of his or her eligible children, to access without tuition to a public high school or a separate high school in the school divisions affected.

(4) Where a board of education has a general attendance area policy, the board of education shall apply that policy equally to pupils attending its high schools as a result of the making of a declaration of intention pursuant to this section.

(5) Notwithstanding subsection 182(3), where a pupil attends a public high school or a separate high school as a result of the making of a declaration of intention pursuant to this section, the pupil shall abide by all policies of the board of education of the school division in which that high school is situated, including any policies relating to religious instruction, religious activities and other programs conducted by the high school.

(6) Where the boards of education of the school divisions affected by a declaration of intention made pursuant to this section consider it expedient, they may:

(a) enter into fee-for-service agreements to make payments for tuition to recover the cost of services provided to pupils in accordance with this section;

(b) mutually agree that no charge will be made to recover the cost of services provided to pupils in accordance with this section; or

(c) where no agreement is made pursuant to clause (a) or (b), charge tuition fees in the amounts prescribed in the regulations, but in no case are those tuition fees to be charged to the pupil or to his parent or guardian (1995, c.E-0.2, s.145).

Part B examines the substantive and procedural rights of non-Catholic students through the lens of a recent legal case: the Hall (2002) decision. Although the protagonist in that case was Catholic, the same general arguments with respect to a dissentient student's substantive right to freedom of conscience under section 2(a) of the Canadian Charter of Rights and Freedoms arguably applies.

PART B

The Substantive and Procedural Rights of Non-Catholic Students: The Marc Hall Case

The substantive and procedural rights of non-Catholic students in Catholic schools, with respect to denominational breach – that is a non-Catholic student's breach of an expected norm of the Catholic Church – has not been discussed in the literature. This issue is significant in Canada especially when considered in conjunction with the rights of all under the Canadian Charter of Rights and Freedoms (1982).

In this Part, I briefly introduce the Charter (1982) and then present the facts, interpretive issue, a statement of the rights of the Catholic student who was the protagonist in the case, and then extend the analysis to apply to hypothetical non-Catholic students.

The charter. In Canadian law, parents cannot waive the Charter rights of their children. The children's rights are separate and distinct from their parents. Yet, older children attending Catholic schools have been assumed to have had their Charter rights waived by their parents in so far as is necessary to be admitted and to be part of the Catholic school community. Arguably, Section 1 of the Charter or section 29 would allow for the suspension of those rights due to the nature of the Catholic school and its history prior to confederation (Donlevy, 2005). This is problematic. A high school student who is living in a common law relationship with another student is acting contrary to the norms of the faith in so far as the Catholic school is concerned, but it may not be presumed that he or she has waived any rights under the Charter merely because his or her parents wish it. This results in a legal anomaly. A second area of some concern is in matters of procedural justice. Do the non-Catholic parent and student have the same procedural rights as Catholic parents and students do? It is a matter for discussion.

A recent Canadian case, albeit decided at a relatively low level of court, highlights the difficulties Canadian courts may have with the issue of rights: procedural and substantive, which may be enjoyed by non-Catholic students in Catholic schools, notwithstanding that in the instant case the protagonist was a Catholic student. It is to that case that I now turn.

A Case of Denominational Breach: Marc Hall

In order to understand the possible impact of the following case on non-Catholic student rights it is first necessary to look at its effects upon Catholic students rights when facing administrative action for denominational breach. This section of Chapter Four presents the facts, the interpretive issue, and the Catholic and non-Catholic students' rights issue as stated and derived from the Hall (2002) case in Ontario. Thereafter, this Chapter looks at the concept of Conscience and freedom of conscience within the Catholic school as arguably it is freedom of conscience which will most challenge Catholic schools in relation to the substantive rights of non-Catholic students.

The Facts. The facts of the Marc Hall (2002) case (hereinafter referred to as Hall) are as follows. Mr. Hall, a gay Catholic high school student in an Ontario Catholic school, sought permission from the school principal, Mr. Powers, to have his gay boyfriend accompany him to the school's graduation prom dance as it was "not part of a religious service (such as Mass), . . . not part of the religious education component of the Board's activity, . . . not held on school property, and . . . not educational in nature[1]" (Hall, 2002, p. 318). His request to do so was denied by the school administration, with the concurrence of the local diocese. The local Bishop, Bishop Meagher, took the position that if permission was granted to Mr. Hall it would represent "clear and positive approval not just of the boy's 'orientation' but of his adopting a homosexual lifestyle" (Hall, 2002, p. 329). Moreover, the Board claimed that to comply with Mr. Hall's request "would have been contrary to their understanding of Catholic beliefs . . . [which were] protected by section 93 of the Constitution Act, 1867, and an appropriate exercise of their freedom of religion under section 2(a) of the Charter" (Hall, 2002, p. 313). Mr. Hall sought judicial review of that decision and an injunction to allow him to attend the prom with his gay friend. He claimed that his section 15 Charter rights,[2] freedom of expression, and not to be discriminated against due to his sexual orientation, had been infringed in his being excluded from attending the prom with his gay friend. He claimed, and the court accepted, that he had been excluded from a significant event in his school life due to his sexual orientation.

Mr. Hall sought injunctory relief [3] which is by necessity a truncated trial procedure as the court is required to decide the issue in a timely fashion long before a full trial. In *Hall*, Mr. Justice MacKinnon held that the Plaintiff was entitled to attend the prom with his friend for several reasons:

a) dancing is not a sexual act and thus if it is not a prohibited activity for heterosexual students, it could not be prohibited for homosexual students (Hall, 2002, pp. 319–324);

b) there is more than one position respecting pastoral care regarding homosexuality in the Catholic Church (Hall, 2002, p. 324);

c) on the issues of irreparable injury and balance of convenience, Mr. Hall had more too loose if he did not attend the dance with his friend, than the School board had to loose if it allowed him to do so (Hall, 2002, pp. 325–328);

d) alternatively, even if Bishop Meager's opinion on Church beliefs was authoritative, the School board "failed to consider less restrictive options that would have given due weight to the plaintiff's rights" (Hall, 2002, p. 325).

The court ruled in favor of Mr. Hall, and as the interim relief was injunctory there was no opportunity for the Catholic school board to appeal the decision prior to Mr. Hall attending the prom dance with his friend. However, Hall, albeit decided at the Ontario Superior Court level, raises new issues of interpretation which could affect denominational cause and which may also presage a new area of law, sanctioning Catholic school students for denominational breach.

The Interpretive Issue

Judges come to the bench with what Twinning (1997) calls a personal "stock of knowledge." He says,

> a 'stock of knowledge' does not consist of individually, empirically tested and readily articulated propositions; rather both individually and collectively we have ill-defined agglomerations of beliefs which typically consist of a complex soup of well-grounded information, sophisticated models, anecdotal memories, impressions, stories, myths, wishes, stereotypes, speculations, and prejudices. (pp. 3–4)

Viewed from a secular perspective, which would be within the "stock of knowledge" of the court, Mr. Justice MacKinnon was correct in deciding in favor of Mr. Hall[4] (Donlevy, 2005) as the court correctly pointed out that notwith standing the position of the Catholic Catechism (Catechism n.d.) on homosexuality, and the evidence of Bishop Meagher, there was dissention amongst the rank and file of the Church on this issue. Therefore, it seemed unreasonable to say that there was an overriding authoritative opinion to which Mr. Hall should conform. In other words, the court saw a clear disconnection between what Bishop Meagher said was the authoritative interpretation of the Church's positions on homosexuality as well as his interpretation of the Catholic Catechism and the opinion of some, perhaps a majority, of the laity. This is rather difficult to make sense of as the court also stated,

> It is not the task of a civil court to direct the Principal, the Board, the Roman Catholic Church or its members, or indeed any member of the public as to what his or her religious beliefs ought to be. The separation of church and state is a fundamental principle of our Canadian democracy and our constitutional law. (Hall, 2002, p. 320)

Nevertheless, the court chose to interpret the official Catholic Church's position regarding the ethics of human behavior through an analysis appropriate to a secular institution, with the deciding factor in the decision being the opinions and practices of members of that institution. Was the court's interpretive approach in error? Arguably, yes, as Justice MacKinnon in a prescient moment may have suspected saying, "Even if I am wrong and the Bishop does have authority to articulate new, previously undocumented doctrine, it has not been done here with minimal impairment to Mr. Hall's rights" (Hall, 2002, p. 325).

The court may have been swayed by the horrific stories of homosexuals who had been abused by society for many years. Yet, as Minow (1996) states,

> stories alone do not articulate principles likely to provide consistency in generalizations to guide future action; stories do not generate guides for what to heed or what additional stories to elicit. Stories on their own offer little guidance for evaluating competing stories. (p. 35)

Kronman (1996) further states "stories do not contain within themselves, the criteria for distinguishing the good ones from the bad . . . the moral evaluation of stories must come from the realm of theory" (p. 54).

The belief that the sanction sought to be imposed upon Mr. Hall by the Catholic school was in the same category as those stories of egregious actions by others evidences the danger of such stories at trial. Indeed, Dershowitz (1996) argues against storytelling at trial saying, "when we import the narrative form of storytelling into our legal system, we confuse fiction with fact and endanger the truth-finding function of the adjudicative process" (p.101). His point is that "as Sartre [1964] put it: "When you tell about life . . . you seem to start at the beginning . . . But in reality you have started at the end" (pp. 39-40). This same argument was proffered by the dissent in the Trinity Western case at the Supreme Court of Canada and failed to be persuasive.[5]

The Students' Rights Issue: The Catholic Student

The Catholic Church is well aware that many adolescent students are at an age of personal instability (Congregation, 1988, paras. 10-13). Therefore, Catholic school administrators should have expected that sooner or later a Catholic high school student would challenge the school's authority on the matter of faith and behavior. This is especially so in the area of morality where a high school student may well feel that he or she did not make a personal agreement with the school to act in accord with the moral and ethical tenants of the Catholic Faith as it was a parental decision that caused her or him to attend the Catholic high school. How could the student be expected to submit to an agreement which she or he had not personally consented? Yet, the Catholic school has a clear responsibility to protect the Catholic milieu in and the Catholic ethos of the school.

Thus, a student who is acting in flagrant disregard to the teachings of the Catholic Church such as living in a common-law relationship, living or advocating a homosexual lifestyle (see Congregation for the Doctrine of the Faith, 1986; Catechism, n.d.), or practicing or advocating occultism of any kind, will find himself or herself in direct conflict with the Catholic school administration. Many of these actions are or can be seen as matters of personal conscience and thus solely a personal matter of the student that have been guaranteed by the Charter. A court might well side with such a dissentient Catholic student.[6] This same logic could well apply to a Catholic student who attempts to establish a pro-gay student association within or outside of the Catholic school. The issues of that student's

Charter rights of conscience, speech, and association certainly could come into play in the legal arena. It is true that sections 1 and 29 of the Charter might save the school's right to take action against a Catholic student in denominational breach – but – unlike denominational cause where an adult contractually agrees to abide by the edicts of the Magisterium, the court could decide that no such agreement exists between the Catholic school and the underage Catholic student. A court may decide notwithstanding the Catholic Catechism, and the Magisterium, there is disagreement within the Catholic Faith as it is lived and thus there is room for a wider application of the acceptability of various moral positions within the Catholic school.

The Students' Rights Issue: The Non-Catholic Student

If denominational breach by a Catholic student is legally problematic for Catholic schools, its application to non-Catholic students in Catholic schools could well be a legal nightmare. The relevant questions are (1) is the number of non-Catholic students in Catholic schools sufficiently large enough to pose a possible problem with denominational breach? (2) does the concept of denominational breach apply to non-Catholic students?

In response to the first question the answer is a resounding yes. Mulligan (1999) quotes an Ontario Catholic school chaplain who says, "It is extremely difficult, if not impossible, to maintain, let alone deepen, the Catholic character of the school with . . . a large [32%] non-Catholic population" (p. 182). The Ontario Catholic School Trustees Association (Ontario, 2000) identified what they believed to be one of the "Major Issues Facing Catholic Education" in, *Our Catholic Schools: A Report on Ontario's Catholic Schools & Their Future*,

> many are worried about internal factors that could threaten our existence . . . Many wondered if the *increasing number of non-Catholic students* who are present in the secondary schools would change the tone of the school. (p. 17) [italics added]

Anecdotal evidence suggests that the number of non-Catholic students in Canada's constitutionally protected Catholic separate schools varies widely from district to district and within each district from school to school but that, depending upon the school district, it may be as high as thirty-two percent. Inclusion had become a major issue in Saskatchewan in 2004-2005, as public school districts sought financial compensation for the loss of students to Catholic school systems:

> The Urban Public Boards in Saskatchewan has challenged the government's funding of non-Catholic students attending Catholic schools. This ongoing constitutional challenge would have major implications for Catholic schools not only in Saskatchewan but possibly Canada-wide, should a decision be reached to fund only Catholic students in Catholic schools. Catholic provincial associations and CCSTA are working closely with Saskatchewan

> Catholic School Section on this important issue. (Canadian Catholic School Trustees' Association, 2005)

Moreover, in Saskatoon, Saskatchewan, the Board of Education wrote the Saskatchewan Minister of Education a letter dated October 9, 2001 stating, amongst other things, its concern regarding the impact a Catholic high school was having upon non-Catholic families in that "at least 300 non-Catholic students attend St. Joseph [the Catholic high school] . . . We are also concerned that our elementary school enrolments . . . suffer because some non-Catholic parents have decided to start their young people in Catholic elementary schools. . . ."

In Western Australia, the Catholic Bishops have restricted the number of non-Catholic students to twenty-five percent of the student population in an attempt to address the issue of Catholicity in Catholic schools. The phenomenon of inclusion is significant both in numbers and to the ethos of Catholic schools. Francis and Gibson (2001) state, "The presence of non-Catholic pupils may . . . have a deleterious impact on the overall school ethos as reflected in the attitude toward Christianity of the student body as a whole" (p. 18).

Having responded affirmatively to the first issue the second need to be addressed, "does the concept of denominational breach apply to non-Catholic students?" I suggest that the answer to that question leads to a) an examination of Canadian juridical concept of freedom of conscience, and b) an understanding of the term conscience within the Catholic Church, and c) the Catholic Church's belief in the exercise of freedom of conscience by non-Catholics within the Catholic school. It is to those areas that I now turn.

PART C

Conscience and the Catholic Church

This section of this book is quite long. In order to understand the connection between the concept of freedom of conscience under section 2(a) of the Charter and the understanding of conscience within the Catholic Church, and how those two areas relate to the non-Catholic student's right to freedom of conscience within the Catholic school a substantial base of information must be provided to the reader. Therefore, what follows outlines the Canadian juridical understanding of freedom of Conscience, the historical and present understandings of the Christian conscience as described through the writings of St. Thomas Aquinas, documents from Vatican II, and several scholastic authorities: Germain Grisez (1983, 1989, Man-in-Relation-to-Law model), Bernard Haring (1963, 1970, 1978, Restless-Heart-Toward-God model), and Cardinal Ratzinger (1991): as he then was). Lastly, the implications of the Charter and the Catholic Church's understandings of conscience are discussed with reference to how they relate to Catholic schools and both Catholic and non-Catholic students (Donlevy, 2008c).

The juridical conscience. Prior to 1982, the Dominion of Canada, following the British model of constitutional law, did not have a written set of constitutional rights and freedoms for its citizens, excepting the Canadian Bill of Rights (1960), which was largely ineffective as it was not a constitutional document, applied only to federal legislation, and was read-down by the courts. Therefore, Canadians were left to trust in the democratic process and common law to protect their rights as citizens in relation to the state. That situation changed in 1982.

Although various constitutional documents had been under the control of the Government of Canada, the Dominion's founding document, the British North America Act, 1867, being a statute of the United Kingdom was under the legislative prevue of that country. In 1982, at the request of the Canadian government, the Parliament of the United Kingdom renamed the BNA Act, 1867 the Constitution Act, 1867 and passed the Canada Act. Attached to the latter was Schedule B, the Canadian Charter of Rights and Freedoms (the Charter). The Charter stated, among other things, that all persons had the right under section 2(a) to "Freedom of conscience and religion" ostensibly only limited by two sections: section 1 where such limitations were according to law and were "demonstrably justifiable in a free and democratic society," and section 33, the *notwithstanding clause*, which allowed the federal and provincial legislatures to temporarily suspend fundamental rights and freedoms and other rights with respect to specific legislation when articulated therein. Although the notwithstanding clause has been used with respect to some issues – such as language rights by the Government of the Province of Quebec – it has never been used with respect to section 2(a): freedom of conscience and religion.

Within short order, the Supreme Court of Canada was asked to adjudicate in a matter dealing with freedom of conscience under section 2(a) of the Charter. In R. v. Big M Drug Mart (1985), the Court heard a matter dealing with store closures and religious holidays. Chief Justice Dickson delivered the majority decision and, in doing so, defined the framework of section 2(a); its conjoint nature, freedom, and the role and significance of conscience in Canadian society.

First, he stated that, "freedom of conscience and religion" form a "single integrated concept" (para. 120) and that when claimed, such freedom, in the Berlinian (2002) sense of positive and negative freedom, "embraces both the absence of coercion and constraint, and the right to manifest beliefs and practices" (para 95; see Donlevy, 2004 for a discussion of negative and positive liberty).
Second he stated that

> freedom means that, subject to such limitations as are necessary to protect public safety, order, health, or morals or the fundamental rights and freedoms of others, no one is to be forced to act in a way contrary to his beliefs or his conscience . . . A truly free society is one which can accommodate a wide variety of beliefs, diversity of tastes and pursuits, customs and codes of conduct. A free society is one which aims at equality with respect to the enjoyment of fundamental freedoms. (para. 95)

Third, the role of conscience and its significance to Canada as a free and democratic society was stated.

> It is because of the centrality of the rights associated with freedom of individual conscience both to basic beliefs about human worth and dignity and to a free and democratic political system that American jurisprudence has emphasized the primacy or 'firstness' of the First Amendment. It is this same centrality that in my view underlies their designation in the Canadian Charter of Rights and Freedoms as 'fundamental.' They are the sine qua non of the political tradition underlying the Charter. . . It should also be noted . . . that an emphasis on individual conscience and individual judgment also lies at the heart of our democratic political tradition. The ability of each citizen to make free and informed decisions is the absolute prerequisite for the legitimacy, acceptability, and efficacy of our system of self-government. (para. 122)

If there was a concern regarding the Chief Justice's comment it may have been with his characterization that the phrase "freedom of conscience and religion" was to be read conjointly. However, later cases from the same court have revised that understanding and determined that although the elements of religion and conscience may be read conjunctively in certain cases that need not necessarily be so as freedom of conscience could stand alone as a fundamental freedom.

The Court was soon to define conscience in juridical terms and to find freedom of conscience as a derivative right under another section of the Charter, section 7. In 1988 in R. v. Morgentaler (1988), the Supreme Court dealt with the prosecution of a Canadian doctor who set-up an abortion clinic to perform abortions for women who had not obtained a certificate from a hospital's therapeutic abortion committee as required by s. 251(4) of the *Criminal Code* of Canada. The Court said,

> The principal issue raised by this appeal . . . [was] whether the abortion provisions of the *Criminal Code*, R.S.C. 1970, c. C-34, infringe the "right to life, liberty and security of the person and the right not to be deprived thereof except in accordance with the principles of fundamental justice" as formulated in s. 7 of the *Canadian Charter of Rights and Freedoms*. (R. v. Morgentaler, 1998, p. 45)

In a split decision, the majority of the Supreme Court found in favour of the appellant doctor for one or more of three reasons: section 251(4) of the Criminal Code breached a woman's right to "life, liberty and security of the person and the right not to be deprived thereof except in accordance with the principles of fundamental justice" (Charter, section 7); section 251(4) breached the appellant's right to freedom of conscience under 2(a) of the Charter; and section 251(4) contained rules unnecessary to the protection of the foetus which alone was sufficient to rule in favour of the appellant doctor. Mr. Justice Wilson, in the majority, noted that in depriving a citizen of section 7 rights the state also deprived her of the right to freedom of conscience. Moreover, he posited that the application of freedom of conscience applied more extensively than only to religious beliefs.

The deprivation of the s. 7 right in this case offends freedom of conscience guaranteed in s. 2(*a*) of the *Charter*. The decision whether or not to terminate a pregnancy is essentially a moral decision and in a free and democratic society the conscience of the individual must be paramount to that of the state. Indeed, s. 2(*a*) makes it clear that this freedom belongs to each of us individually.

> Freedom of conscience and religion' should be broadly construed to extend to conscientiously-held beliefs, whether grounded in religion or in a secular morality and the terms 'conscience' and 'religion' should not be treated as tautologous if capable of independent, although related, meaning. The state here is endorsing one conscientiously-held view at the expense of another. It is denying freedom of conscience to some, treating them as means to an end, depriving them of their 'essential humanity. (p. 37)

The significance of the Big M and Morgentaler cases are that the Court had defined freedom of conscience not as the collective right of a community but as an individual right, in accord with Dworkin's (1977) notion of rights, in that it was necessary to ensure a free, liberal democracy. Further, juridically, conscience was based upon a secular liberal definition of conscience as "conscientiously held beliefs."

Notwithstanding the above, the Court was not prepared to give free reign to freedom of conscience within the individual sphere of action. In Rodriguez v. British Columbia (Attorney General) (1993), a terminally ill patient suffered from an advanced state of amyotrophic lateral sclerosis and sought to be provided assistance at a future stage of the illness in order to commit suicide as she would be incapable of the act herself. Section 241(b) of the Criminal Code of Canada prohibited the giving of assistance to commit suicide. A majority of the Court held that the section 7 Charter rights of "life, liberty and security of the person" were to be balanced against the consciously held belief of the individual and further that the section 7 rights reflected and represented a value in Canadian society – the sanctity of life. On balancing the individual's right to freedom of conscience and society's value of the sanctity of life and further as there was no consensus in Canadian society respecting the acceptance of assisted suicide, the Court concluded that the relevant section of the Criminal Code was intra vires and denied the appellant patient her remedy.

In dissent, Chief Justice Lamer, would have allowed the patient to take her own life with assistance and stated that commonly held religious beliefs should not preclude the operation of an individual's freedom of conscience. He stated,

> In my opinion, the Court should answer this question without reference to the philosophical and theological considerations fuelling the debate on the morality of suicide or euthanasia. It should consider the question before it from a legal perspective . . . while keeping in mind that the Charter has established the essentially secular nature of Canadian society and the central place of freedom of conscience in the operation of our institutions. (p. 366)

Yet, it was clear that the majority had considered secular reasons in its decision as Mr. Justice Sopinka stated, "Aiding or counseling a person to commit suicide, on the one hand, and homicide, on the other, are sometimes extremely closely related" (p. 55). Arguably, the possibility of abuse and the lack of a political consensus in favour of assisted suicide were the secular reasons for the Court's judgment. That suggested conclusion is also in concert with Lamer's comment in Rodriguez (1993) where he said that the Canadian Charter, "has established the essentially secular nature of Canadian society and the central place of freedom of conscience in the operation of our institutions" (p. 366).

The current Chief Justice of the Supreme Court appears, (McLachlin, 2005), in a broad sense, to agree with that statement when she stated that,

> There is no doubt that . . . government by consent, the protection of life and personal security, and freedom from discrimination – can all be advanced by moral argument. It is worth noting, however, that they can also be supported by a democratic argument grounded in conceptions of the state and fundamental human dignity that we have developed since John Stuart Mill . . . the legitimacy of the modern democratic state arguably depends on its adhesion to fundamental norms that transcend the law and executive action. . . . (p. 3)

Notwithstanding the above, it is certainly arguable that the juridical conscience can rest its justification upon religious beliefs in a liberal, pluralistic, democracy. Taylor (1995) notes,

> The secular is grounded on common action not religious beliefs but there is no reason why religious beliefs might not form such a common action. The key seems to be that one should not assume that the secular society should exclude the religious in so far as a liberal democratic pluralistic society is concerned. (p. 309)

In other words, conscience is the broader concept under which conscientiously held religious beliefs would qualify as requiring freedom, not the converse.

Benson (1999-2000) offers three definitions of the secular from Canadian case law which this book adopts:

- The state is expressly non-religious and must not support religion in any way ("neural" secular);
- The state does not affirm religious belies of any particular religious group but may act so as to create conditions favorable to religions generally ("positive" secular);
- The state is not competent in matters involving religion but must not act so as to inhibit religious manifestations that do not threaten the common good ("negative "secular). (p. 530)

The thorny question remained how an adjudicator could determine the bona fides of a belief when it was not religiously based. The Federal Court of Canada (Trial Division) dealt with that question in Maurice v. Canada (Attorney General) (2002).

In Maurice a prison inmate made application for special consideration regarding a lacto-vegetarian diet which the prison officials had refused. He claimed that as other prisoners' special diets had been granted based upon religious reasons, he too should have such consideration for reasons of conscience under section 2(a) of the Charter. His application was successful. Justice Campbell held that,

> cogent evidence must be produced to prove the conscientious belief to a balance of probabilities. On the evidence in the present case, I have no difficulty finding that the Applicant does have a strongly held belief regarding the consumption of animal products. (p. 1)

The "cogent evidence" clearly referred to not just an articulated belief but also a behavioral pattern which lent credibility to the individual's actions.

Mention should be made, as Mr. Justice Campbell stated in Maurice (2002), that under Article 18 of the United Nations Universal Declaration of Human Rights freedom of conscience is mentioned and further that Canada is a signatory to that document. However, such international documents – ratified only by the executive branch of government – are not law in Canada – although the Supreme Court has held that they may be philosophically persuasive (Baker, 1999).

The above cases establish some of the parameters of freedom of conscience under the Canadian Charter of Rights and Freedoms. Juridically, freedom of conscience is a fundamental right of all persons, it is expressly protected under section 2(a) but may be derived from section 7 (Rodriguez, 1993); it is defined as a belief conscientiously or strongly held (R. v. Big M, 1985; Maurice, 2002); it is an individual right not a collective right (R. v. Big M, 1985); it requires a cogent manifestation and clear indicia that such a belief is bona fide held by the individual (Maurice, 2002); it is not based upon a philosophy, or theology but arguably it may be so (R. v. Morgentaler, 1988; McLachlin, 2005); its expression must be balanced against the fundamental rights and values of the Charter (Rodriguez, 1993); and it is warranted as one of the, if not the, keystones to a free, democratic, pluralistic, democracy. The above is consistent with the idea that the Charter's rights and freedoms are interpreted by the courts by the *purposive method* which takes into account the purpose and rationale of the freedom or right in question within the context of the Charter as a whole, the Canadian legal and political tradition, and the changing needs of Canadian society (Adler v. Ontario, 1996; O.*E.C.T.A. v. Ontario* (Attorney General), 2001, para 32). Juridically, freedom of conscience is the sine qua non of a free, democratic, pluralistic, liberal society (R. v. Big M, 1985).

I would be remiss not to briefly mention that the term conscience has been employed in cases which have not been concerned with freedom of conscience in order to ascertain if their usage of that term is relevant to this paper. The conclusion of this author is that such cases may have some relevance. Some Canadian cases have spoken of matters which "shock the conscience." In particular, that juridical expression has been used in matters of fundamental justice where the extradition of a foreign fugitive from Canada to a state wherein the accused might face extremely harsh treatment is seen as contrary to Canadian values (Canada v.

Schmidt, 1987, para 47; United States v. Burns, 2001, para. 66; Suresh v. Canada (Minister of Citizenship and Immigration) 2002; Gwynne v. Canada (Minister of Justice), 1998, p. 13). It thus appears that conscience has, in at least some cases, perhaps under section 7 of the Charter, a collective meaning not as a fundamental freedom but rather as an interpretive principle in relation to the Charter's legal rights.

Moreover, the relevance and importance of conscience has been cited in Canadian law with regard to the application of the principles of equity. Therein it can, when there is convergence with an equitable principle or in the case of unconscionability, successfully establish a ground for an action: constructive trust (Rathwell v. Rathwell, 1978; Pettkus v. Becker, 1980), implied trust, compensation for error in law, and mistake in law as well as other equitable grounds. In Soulos v. Korkontzilas, (1997) McLachlin cited with approval the statement by McClean (Rathwell v. Rathwell, 1978, p. 169) "Good conscience . . . lies at the very foundation of equitable jurisdiction" (para. 27). Conscience in Equity is a complex area beyond the scope of this paper; however, upon reading the mentioned cases; one is left wondering whose conscience the courts are referring to? Is it the court's conscience, the public's conscience, a party's conscience, a philosophical definition of conscience, or a theological definition of conscience? In any event, case law points to the relevance, perseverance, and significance of the idea of conscience in Canadian jurisprudence.

In sum, the juridical conscience in Canada is intrinsically entwined with the concept of freedom and is perceived by the courts as a key stone for a free, democratic, pluralistic society. It is secular in nature and relies upon the history, norms, and values of Canadian society for its content and juridical interpretation, which in turn underpins and legitimizes the authority of the modern democratic state. Moreover, as a concept it is present in matters of extradition and equity and is used as a collective concept for Canadian values acting both as a shield (negative liberty) and a sword (positive liberty) for the individual.

The Christian Conscience

Generally on conscience. There have been many scholarly works which have been written on conscience which encompass the history of the concept from the Greeks (Apuleius, 1984); through Judaism and biblical sources (Gorsky, 1999) to modern times touching upon other views: Catholic (Delhayne, 1968), Protestant (Robbins, 1978; Leal, 1999), Orthodox (Thomas, 1999), Islam (Geaves, 1999), Buddhism (Chryssides, 1999), Hinduism (Sharma, 2004), psychology (Freud, 1923), and biology (Carey, 2007). Such an historical overview is obviously beyond this book.

Suffice to say that every human being is faced with decisions which she or he perceives as a choice between right and wrong, good and bad, or bad and bad. It is also true that the individual in that position will attempt to exercise some understanding, no matter how rudimentary, of right and wrong, good and bad, or bad and worse. Further, once having made the decision, it will be open to future scrutiny by the individual with respect to its coherence with the criteria upon which it was chosen.

This section of this book asks, from a Catholic perspective, from what source does the desire to choose the right or the good derive, how does one determine the content which allows one to determine the right from the wrong, and lastly through what process can one make that determination? Aquinas (1948), Vatican II (1965a, 1965b), Grisez (1983), Haring (1970), and Ratzinger (2007) have provided some guidance with respect to those questions.

Aquinas on Conscience

St. Thomas Aquinas is the touchstone for Roman Catholic thought on the conception of conscience; his views will be briefly reviewed.

For Aquinas, the faculty of reason is inherent to all humans and allows the individual to comprehend the natural law which is created and directed by God. Moreover, reason encompasses not just the intellectual faculty of the mind but also all other ways of knowing. He posits that by human nature all people seek the good and avoid the evil as an unerring, innate condition of being human. This innate condition is called synderesis and as Aquinas says:

> In order that there can be some rightness in human deeds, there must be some enduring principle which has unchangeable rightness and by reference to which all deeds are tested, such that this enduring principle resists everything evil and gives assent to everything good. This is what synderesis is, whose job is to murmur back in reply to evil and to turn us towards what is good. Hence, it is to be admitted that it can not do wrong. (Aquinas, 1980)[7]

Having established a basic element in being human as a tendency towards the good, Aquinas moves on to what he terms conscience. He considers conscience an act not a power as it "denotes knowledge ordered towards something, since it means knowledge-along-with-another. But applying knowledge to something is an act. So from the name it is clear that conscience is an act" (Aquinas, 1948, pp. 407–408) which can be in error as it is the application of the a priori principle of the good known in synderesis to a particular, contextual situation. Aquinas is clear that although one must follow one's conscience, merely doing so will not guarantee the correct choice but such will ensure that sin will not be incurred (Aquinas, 1980, p. 54). Nevertheless, even in error, he says "[w]ithout any doubt, *conscientia* binds" (Aquinas, 1980, p. 54). He explains this proposition, saying

> to believe in Christ is good in itself and necessary for salvation; all the same this does not win the will unless it is recommended by reason. If the reason presents it as bad, then the will reaches to it in the light, not that it is really bad in itself, but because it appears so because of a condition that happens to be attached by the reason apprehending it. (Aquinas, 1948, p. 675)

However, willful blindness results in moral culpability as,

> If the reason or conscience err with an error that is voluntary, either directly, or through negligence, so that one errs about what one ought to know; then such an error of reason or conscience does not excuse the will, that abides by that erring reason or conscience, from being evil. (Aquinas, 1948, p. 676)

The difficulty is that one has no assurance that one's conscience is unerring when making a moral decision. However, Aquinas offers certain resources for the conscience to assist in alleviating that concern: prudence and its accompanying virtues, the gifts of the Holy Spirit, and connaturality. Those three resources bridge the gap between the unerring synderesis and fallible act of conscience.

The assisting virtues of prudence are: the ability to take counsel, sound or practical judgment according to accepted rules of conduct, and the intelligence to judge exceptional cases outside of the norm (Aquinas, 1948). The gifts of the Holy Spirit incorporate wisdom, knowledge, understanding, counsel, fortitude, piety, and fear, which corresponded to and assist the fundamental element of conscience – prudence. Connaturality includes all ways of knowing beyond the intellectual and as Aquinas (1948) says:

> [W]isdom denotes a certain rightness of judgment in accord with divine principles. Now rightness of judgment is twofold: first, in accord with the complete use of reason, second, on account of a certain connaturality with the matter about which one has to judge. Thus, about matters of chastity, a man after inquiring with his reason forms a right judgment, if he has acquired the knowledge of ethics, while the one who has the virtue of chastity judges of such matter by a kind of connaturality. Accordingly it belongs to the wisdom that is an intellectual virtue to pronounce right judgment about divine things after reason has made its inquiry, but it belongs to wisdom as a gift of the Holy Spirit to judge aright about them on account of connaturality with them. (Summa Theologiae, pt. II-II Q. 45, art. 2)

As May (2003) states, "connatural knowledge is . . . a knowledge resulting from an interaction between sensitivity and affectivity, intellect and will, knowing and loving" (p. 228). In sum, for Aquinas the inherent and unerring synderesis acts in conjunction with prudence which produces the act of conscience in order to produce a morally inculpable decision. Honest error does not make that decision culpable.

If, notwithstanding the above, the individual comes to a conscientious decision which seems in error to others, even the *Catholic Magisterium*, then Aquinas says, "anyone upon whom the ecclesiastical authorities, in ignorance of the true facts, impose a demand that offends against his clear conscience, should perish in excommunication rather than violate his conscience" (St. Thomas Aquinas, 2006).

That statement was grist for the topic of conscience at Vatican II, the documents of which indicate that Aquinas's' view of conscience has been interpreted, in part, in different ways.

The Documents of Vatican II

The term conscience was frequently referred to in the documents of Vatican II although its meaning varied upon the intention of the Church Fathers and at times within the context of the purpose of the documents (Halstead, 1986).

Certainly conscience was on the mind of the Church Fathers as in *Gaudium et Spes* they noted that:

> In the depths of his conscience, man detects a law which he does not impose upon himself, but which holds him to obedience. Always summoning him to love good and avoid evil, the voice of conscience when necessary speaks to his heart: do this, shun that. For man has in his heart a law written by God; to obey it is the very dignity of man; according to it he will be judged. Conscience is the most secret core and sanctuary of a man. There he is alone with God, Whose voice echoes in his depths. (Vatican II, 1965c, para. 16)

This theme on the "reciprocity of conscience and the inviolable dignity and freedom of the individual conscience" (Hoose, 1999) was also reflected in the *Declaration on Religious Freedom*, which stresses inquiry and dialogue within the community of believers in the individual's search for truth:

> Truth, however, is to be sought after in a manner proper to the dignity of the human person and his social nature. The inquiry is to be free, carried on with the aid of teaching or instruction, communication and dialogue, in the course of which men explain to one another the truth they have discovered, or think they have discovered, in order thus to assist one another in the quest for truth. (p. 62)

Moreover, as the truth is discovered, it is by a personal assent that men are to adhere to it (Vatican II, 1965a).

Again, the Church stresses both the freedom and the binding nature of the individual's conscience:

> On his part, man perceives and acknowledges the imperatives of the divine law through the mediation of conscience. In all his activity a man is bound to follow his conscience in order that he may come to God, the end and purpose of life. It follows that he is not to be forced to act in manner contrary to his conscience. Nor, on the other hand, is he to be restrained from acting in accordance with his conscience, especially in matters religious. The reason is that the exercise of religion, of its very nature, consists before all else in those internal, voluntary and free acts whereby man sets the course of his life directly toward God. No merely human power can either command or prohibit acts of this kind. (Vatican II, 1965a, para. 3)

Yet the Church Fathers went on to say in Article 14 that the correct formation of the individual conscience is crucial:

> [i]n the formation of their consciences, the Christian faithful ought carefully to attend to the sacred and certain doctrine of the Church. For the Church is,

> by the will of Christ, the teacher of the truth. It is her duty to give utterance to, and authoritatively to teach, that truth which is Christ Himself, and also to declare and confirm by her authority those principles of the moral order which have their origins in human nature itself. (Vatican II, para. 14)

As Gleesen (2003) notes, one finds in *Gaudium et Spes*, Article 16, and one could argue Articles 3 and 14 of *Dignitatis Humanae Personae,* that, those texts

> [i]nvoke both legalistic and religious understandings of conscience. It directs our attention both to the objectivity of the moral law and to the unique and inviolable character of a person's response to God's call. What the text does not do is explain how these two realities are to be understood in relation to each other.

Speaking further on conscience, in *Lumen Gentium* the Fathers noted in Article 16 that those who are open to synderesis and yet who do not know the Gospel are not culpable for their lack of belief. The Fathers said,

> Those . . . who through no fault of their own do not know the Gospel of Christ or His Church, yet sincerely seek God and moved by grace strive by their deeds to do His will as it is known to them through the dictates of conscience. Nor does Divine Providence deny the helps necessary for salvation to those who, without blame on their part, have not yet arrived at an explicit knowledge of God and with His grace strive to live a good life. Whatever good or truth is found amongst them is looked upon by the Church as a preparation for the Gospel. She knows that it is given by Him who enlightens all men so that they may finally have life. (Vatican II, 1964a, para. 16)

The Fathers further re-stated Aquinas's position that listening to conscience develops an abiding moral sense of right and wrong which becomes habitual and may be known as the Christian Conscience ("*conscientia Christiana*") which is then manifest in certain behaviors – love of neighbor, service projects, and the like – and forbids others (Halstead, 1986). It is of significance for the aspect of this chapter on Catholic education that the Vatican II document *Gravissimum Educationis*, should be noted. In that document the Church Fathers stressed both students' and parents' freedom of conscience declaring, "that children and young people have a right to be motivated to appraise moral values with a right conscience, to embrace them with a personal adherence, together with a deeper knowledge and love of God" (Vatican II, 1965b, para. 1). It went on to say that it was this freedom which

> contributes in the highest degree to the protection of freedom of conscience, the rights of parents, as well as to the betterment of culture itself . . . Let them do all they can to stimulate their students to act for themselves . . . . (para. 8)

Another Vatican II document, *Apostolicam Actuositatem*, stressed the importance for the individual of not a specific moral decision but rather "a general moral outlook"

(Halstead, 1986) and "not as some bishops wished, the reality of the objective world and the objective moral order."

As Halstead correctly points out the documents of Vatican II do not reduce the apparent ambiguity between the personal duty in the individual to form her or his own conscience and the individual's responsibility to listen to the church, its tradition, and Magisterium. It is certainly correct to say that "the Council fathers . . . were willing to tolerate two different visions of the moral life" (p. 133). Cardinal Ratzinger points to the conundrum when speaking of the two interpretations:

> One is a renewed understanding of the Catholic essence, which expounds Christian faith from the basis of freedom and as the very principle of freedom itself. The other is a superseded, 'pre-conciliar' model, which subjects Christian existence to authority, regulating life even in its most intimate preserves, and thereby attempts to maintain control over people's lives. Morality of conscience and morality of authority, as two opposing models, appear to be locked in struggle with each other. Accordingly, the freedom of the Christian would be rescued by appeal to the classical principle of moral tradition: That conscience is the highest norm that man is to follow, even in opposition to authority. Authority – in this case, the Magisterium – may well speak of matters moral, but only in the sense of presenting conscience with material for its own deliberation. Conscience would retain, however, the final word. Some authors reduce conscience in this, its aspect of final arbiter to the formula "conscience is infallible" . . . but . . . if this were the case, it would mean that there is no truth—at least not in moral or religious matters, which is to say, in the areas that constitute the very pillars of our existence. (Ratzinger, 1991, also Ratzinger, 2007, pp. 11-12)

Further attempts by the Church were made to clarify the issues, and perhaps to resolve at least one problem. *Veritatis Spendor* (John Paul II, 1993) dealt with the difficulty with proportionalism, which states that "whether there are some kinds of action (such as the use of contraception) which are 'always wrong,' no matter what the circumstances or intentions of the people the involved" (Gleeson, 2003) but the tension remained between the two quite different interpretations of conscience both claiming the Aquinas' inheritance. In particular, one author saw *Veritatis Spendor* as attempting to reinforce the Magisterium's primacy (Harvey, 1994).

The documents of Vatican II state that the Catholic Church's position is that there is an objective moral truth based upon natural law provided by God and which can provide guidance to human action. That truth is known through reason, the tradition of the Church, and the Magisterium which is guided by the Holy Spirit. The individual desires (synderesis) to seek the truth in moral deliberations by applying reason and prudence, with its various assistants, to the contextualized situation within which the moral decision is to be made. The individual conscience may err and not be morally culpable but she or he must have applied prudence both to the content and decision-making process.

Nevertheless, the issue of authority versus autonomy and freedom remains a question on the Catholic Church's understanding of conscience. Fundamentally, the difficulty was with what Smith (1998) calls the revisionist and no-revisionist approaches to conscience. It is to a brief overview of those two positions that I now turn.

The Revisionist and No-Revisionist Approaches

Two Catholic writers, Germain Grisez and Bernard Haring, each represent a differing view of conscience, both claiming the Aquinas inheritance.

The Man-in-Relation-to-Law Model (Germain Grisez)

Grisez's non-revisionism has been called the "man-in-relation-to-law" approach (Smith, 1998). Grisez begins with the notion that no action has moral praise or culpability in terms of the individual unless it is freely chosen. It is the radical freedom of the autonomous individual to freely choose which makes the actor's action, in terms of the actor, moral or immoral. Indeed, for Grisez (1983), conscience is "an awareness of mortal truth" (p. 74). He suggests that the colloquial understanding of conscience is in three parts, which is consistent with Aquinas' understanding: an awareness of moral principles, the analysis of a particular situation based upon those principles, and the action or inaction taken. Further, he is in agreement with Aquinas that conscience must be followed, but suggests that the Magisterium of the Catholic Church has bridged the gap between the moral principles written on the soul by natural law and their application in the contextually created lives of individuals. Hence, the individual conscience should follow all particulars of action and inaction as delineated by the Magisterium. Connaturality has its place if a person is mature and prudent, which in turn will bring that person to accept the teachings of the Magisterium. As the Catholic Church is guided by the Holy Spirit, the "faithful and clearheaded Catholic [has] . . . no right to follow a judgment of conscience against the teaching of the magisterium" (Grisez, 1999; 1989, 56 Linacve Q. 13, 17).

The "Restless-Heart-Toward-God" Model (Bernard Haring)

Haring's revisionism has been called the "restless-heart-toward-God" model (Smith, 1998). His moral framework is complex and goes well beyond this paper, but the major elements of his view of conscience should be mentioned. For Haring, the human conscience appears to be an innate human capacity which is oriented towards the good and is driven by its freedom to search for the truth of that good within relationships – indeed, within community – while employing prudence in actions within particular circumstances. The importance of the community is that "man's conscience is unthinkable without an active sharing of experiences and insights with others searching for truth in mutual responsibility" (Haring, 1970,

p. 69). It is prudence, which is developed through a relationship with God, which provides a clear view of that which is the instant case facing the person and which suggests the correct course of action. He states, "The virtue of prudence can flourish only in the soil of sound conscience" (Haring, 1963, p. 510). For Haring, conscience is "the inner core, the deepest wellspring of integration and wholeness" (Haring, 1978, p. 259).

His view is that the "mere inculcation of various doctrines, without a synthesis in Christ and without a sharing of the faith, does nothing to help the formation of a distinctly Christian conscience . . . [and] can become an obstacle to an integrated faith"(p. 259). He goes on to say that "it staggers the imagination to think that an earthly authority or an ecclesiastical Magisterium could take away from man his own decision of conscience" (p. 63).

Although Haring appreciates the significance of the Magisterium, he takes the position that the Church has long sought obedience before conscience and that "in the face of such authority . . . a considerable distrust of any command is an obligation of conscience" (Haring, 1967, p. 60).

Pope Benedict XVI

Cardinal Ratzinger, as earlier stated, weighed into the discussion saying that the "morality of conscience and morality of authority, as two opposing models, appear to be locked in struggle with each other" (Ratzinger, 2007, p. 12; see also Ratzinger 1991). His concern seems to be that a "firm, subjective conviction and the lack of doubts . . . do not justify man . . . [in that] the Pharisee no longer knows that he too has guilt. He has a completely clear conscience . . . Their consciences no longer accuse them but justify them" (pp. 17, 19).

His understanding is that:

> Two standards become apparent for ascertaining the presence of a real voice of conscience. First, conscience is not identical to personal wishes and taste. Second, conscience cannot be reduced to social advantage, to group consensus, or to the demands of political and social power . . . historically considered, morality does not belong to the area of subjectivity, but is guaranteed by the community and has a reference to the community. (Ratzinger, 2007, p. 53)

Cardinal Ratzinger seems to answer the question of the conscience in apparent conflict with the Magisterium by conflating the two through the concept of truth. That is, neither conscience nor the teachings of the Church are in conflict with the truth. The former looks to remembrance "not only of the moral law written on our hearts but also to a teaching on conscience that is true to our deepest traditions and to our own humanity" (Haas, 2007).

It appears that Cardinal Ratzinger offers that synderesis directs one towards the truth, and that prudence and its associates orient one towards the truth which involves the freedom to search within the tradition of the faith and the faith community in dialogue with a mature, respectful, serious, and hence bona fide consideration of the teachings of the Magisterium. Once the search is complete the individual's conscience must act in accord with its own understanding whatever the cost. That cost may be high and will not necessarily bring the conscience into conflict with the Magisterium but when that is so, one's own conscience must be obeyed before all else, if necessary even against the requirement of ecclesiastical authority. This emphasis on the individual, whose conscience confronts him with a supreme and ultimate tribunal, is one which in the last resort is beyond the claim of external social groups, even of the official Church (Ratzinger, 1969).

Cardinal Ratzinger's position is in accord with that of Cardinal Newman who, when in a letter to the Duke of Norfolk, wrote, "If I am obliged to bring religion into after dinner toasts (which indeed does not seem to be quite right) I shall drink to the Pope, if you please – still, to conscience first, and to the Pope afterwards" (Ratzinger, 2007). His position is also consistent with that of John Paul II in his Message "On the Value and Content of Conscience and Religion" delivered in 1980.

In summary, although there appears to be a conflict within the Catholic idea of conscience between authority and autonomy that dichotomy may be an error. What appears to be at issue is neither the conscience as action, nor the specific content upon which that action is based, but rather the importance of prudence and its associates in the selection of the contents of one's conscience and the mature reflective process through which the individual arrives at a consciously held decision.

The understandings of conscience are important for its freedom within Catholic schools.

IMPLICATIONS FOR FREEDOM OF CONSCIENCE IN CATHOLIC SCHOOLS

This part of this book summarizes the juridical and current Catholic views of freedom of conscience and describes the difficulties which Catholic school administrators face in applying a Catholic definition of conscience within Catholic schools.

The Juridical Concept

The juridical concept of freedom of conscience in the Canadian Charter of Rights and Freedoms offers a view founded upon a free, democratic, pluralistic, and liberal society which requires its citizens to make their own choices about fundamental matters involving how they wish to live their lives within that society (Donlevy, 2008). The State is committed to the protection of citizens' consciences from the tyranny of the majority, if the beliefs which underlie those choices are "conscientiously-held beliefs" and do not, in their expression, deleteriously affect others.

Moreover, freedom of conscience may also be derived, in part, from the legal right to liberty and security of the person under section 7 of the Charter (Donlevy, 2008). The individual's conscience is thus viewed externally by the state as the necessary motor for individual choice, not to be restricted by the state except in balancing others' rights (under section 1) or temporarily suspended (under section 33).

The Sacred Concept

The Catholic Church's view of conscience as articulated in the writings of St. Thomas Aquinas and the documents of Vatican II can be interpreted as incorporating two models: "Man in Relation to Law" and "Restless-Heart-Toward-God." The distinction between the models is the extent of the authoritative role of the Magisterium not only in the formation of the individual's antecedent conscience but also in the culpability of the consequential conscience.

Freedom of Conscience and Catholic Schools

The legal issue. As earlier stated, in Canada, there are three provinces that have constitutionally protected Catholic schools, which receive funding from those provinces: Ontario, Alberta, and Saskatchewan. The rights and privileges of Catholic schools in those provinces, which were acknowledged in law prior to each province entering confederation, are constitutionally entrenched and may only be abrogated through a constitutional process. Further, those rights and privileges may not be deleteriously affected by the rights and freedoms within the Canadian Charter of Rights and Freedoms as section 29 of the Charter states "[n]othing in this Charter abrogates or derogates from any rights or privileges guaranteed by or under the Constitution of Canada in respect of denominational, separate or dissentient schools" (Canadian Charter of Rights and Freedoms, 1982). This section of the Charter refers to legal rights which existed prior to the geographical area becoming a province. Therefore, the right of Catholic schools to demand remediation or to seek dismissal of non-conformists is arguably constitutionally entrenched within the Dominion's constitution.

The legal difficulty arises when a non-conformist Catholic or non-Catholic student or teacher claims the 'Restless-Heart-Towards-God' justification for such non-conformity. In the past, Catholic schools have sought successfully to dismiss teachers for denominational non-conformity. In particular, Catholic teachers who married only in civil ceremonies were dismissed (see Essex Roman Catholic Separate School board, 1978), a Catholic teacher who married a non-Catholic whose divorced marriage had not been annulled was dismissed (see Caldwell v. Stuart, 1985), and an unmarried Catholic teacher who became pregnant was dismissed for non-conformist behavior (see Casagrande v. Hinton, 1987). Moreover, even in non-constitutionally protected Catholic schools in provinces and territories not mentioned above, the Catholic school board has the right to demand denominational conformity and to monitor conformity on a continuous basis (Caldwell v. Stuart, 1985).

Given, however, the two interpretations of conscience within the Catholic Church, a non-conformist, for some acts of non-conformity which are not contrary to the Church's dogma, may claim not only the Church's guaranteed freedom of conscience but also that the conscientious choice, which albeit is not in accord with the teachings of the Magisterium, is nevertheless a choice which does not exclude them from the Church. Hence, remediation of the non-conformity is not appropriate as a demand from school administration nor is dismissal based upon a warranted denominational cause. Arguably, it is not open to Catholic school administrators to say that their decision is defensible by the fact that a majority of the school's Catholic parents do not accept the nonconformity as the religious aspects of the Catholic school fall under the aegis of the Church (Code of Canon Law, 1983) and its definition of freedom and conscience. According to this argument, what is at issue is the individual's exercise of her or his freedom of conscience not the perception of the majority of the laity within a school community.

If the above analysis is correct, then a Catholic school administrator's decision to demand remediation or to dismiss a non-conformist is not denominationally based; therefore, it must be founded in civil law. Such a conclusion means that the decision is not constitutionally protected from scrutiny, and that the Charter rights of the non-conformist are in full force. As the Charter is interpreted using the purposeful method and on a secular basis, non-conformity to a religious creed is not an operative claim, nor can it be claimed to be so by the Catholic Church's own definition of freedom and conscience. Although there are some common law precedents in Labor Law which provide for the remediation of employees' behaviors which draw the employer's business reputation into disrepute and deleteriously affect the business, such do not stand against a constitutional (Charter) right which applies to organs of the state such as the institution of education. Moreover, Section 1 of the Charter is not arguable by the school employer as by the Catholic Church's own definition, students and others have freedom of conscience which may be expressed in the 'Restless-Heart-Towards-God' model.

It has been argued elsewhere that the Hall (2002) decision was wrongly decided on the grounds that the Court misconstrued the teachings of the Catholic Church as being necessarily majoritarian in order to be authoritative (Donlevy, 2005). However, if Hall had claimed that the expression of his sexual orientation was a choice made in good conscience in accord with the 'Restless-Heart-Toward-God' model, he would ostensibly have had a legally unassailable argument. His action, although non-conformist in expression, was within the ambit of denominationally protected freedom of conscience in the Catholic Church.

Traditionally, one might argue that, because the local Bishop gave evidence against Hall's request, a voice of the Magisterium had determined in favor of the school district. Indeed, a local bishop does have authority over Catholic education to ensure "the authentic Christian character of the Catholic school" (Congregation, 1977, para 73) but he does not necessarily always speak as the authoritative voice of the Catholic Church. A local bishop speaks with authority on an issue as a result of, and when in concurrence with, the contents of the official Church documents (John Paul II, 1998). As Feuerherd (2002) states, "Under this 1998 papal apostolic letter, bishops' conference statements that seek to bind the faithful must be approved unanimously, or, with a two-thirds vote, submitted to Rome for approval."

Moreover, although the Code of Canon Law speaks of children and young persons that are to be cared for so they may achieve freedom, that does not discount the warrant for non-conformity which is within the 'Restless-Heart-Towards-God' model. Although many in the Catholic Church might disagree with a non-conformist, the Catechism of the Catholic Church provides that "[a] human being must always obey the certain judgment of his conscience" (Catechism, n.d., para. 1790).

If that is correct, then the question becomes: Are the actions of Catholic and non-Catholic students and teachers who act in accord with their conscience yet contrary to the normally espoused values of Catholic schools subject to administrative remediation and or dismissal? The answer may arguably be no. Why?

The Catholic school is bound to protect the individual's freedom of conscience in terms of religion and the 'Restless to Heart' model provides for a reasonable basis for the non-conformist's action. By the Church's definition, the non-conformist teacher or student acts within the terms of the denomination and not in conflict with it. This appears to be the case notwithstanding the Canadian Conference of Catholic Bishops (1973, December 1) "Statement on the Formation of Conscience". Hence the administrative demand for remediation must be based on civil law. That is problematic, because once outside of the area of constitutional protection for administrative action, it is arguable that the student or teacher's section 2(a) right and all other Charter and civil rights are fully operative is defending non-conformist actions.

SUMMARY

This chapter has provided a summary of two major schools of thought regarding conscience in the Catholic Church. In the first case the argument was made that, although section 2(a) was secular in a juridical sense, the operation of section 29 of the Charter and section 93 of the 1867 Constitution Act provided for a sacred or religious definition of conscience to be read into those constitutional documents. However, it was further argued that by operation of the two interpretations of the Catholic Church's definition of conscience, the Catholic school administrator may not claim such a constitutional shield for the remediation and/or dismissal of non-conformist teachers or students. If that is the case, the ordinary public law applies, which provides the non-conformist with a defense utilizing section 2(a) freedom of conscience in a secular sense under the Charter.

Non-Catholic students retain their Charter rights unaffected by section 93 of the Constitution Act, 1867, and section 29 of the Charter. They are invited into the Catholic school and through the documents of the Catholic Church are provided the right to freedom of conscience and religion as members of the Catholic school community. The Catholic Church is very clear in prescribing the Catholic schools treatment of non-Catholic students, both in that invitation and in ensuring those students' rights to freedom of conscience and religion (Vatican II, 1965b, paras. 2, 9, 10; Vatican II, 1965a, para. 2). As those students are not part of the Catholic Faith community they cannot be expected to be bound by the theological expectations of that Church or the derivative behavioral expectations, excepting as stated in the relevant provincial statute or arguably, in contract.

The Congregation for Catholic Education (1988) stated, "[there are countries where the majority of] the students are not Catholics . . . The religious freedom and the personal conscience of individual students and their families must be respected, and this freedom is explicitly recognized by the Church" (para 6).

Section 1 of the Charter requires that the limitation on a Charter right must be "prescribed in law," hence the requirement that a statutory prohibition or expectation must speak to the behavior of the non-Catholic student in the Catholic school. However, even if that is the case, there remains a wide scope for non-conforming behavior of non-Catholic students which otherwise would be considered a denominational breach and subject to administrative sanctions. Therefore, where a non-Catholic students seeks to utilize her or his section 2 Charter rights of freedom of conscience, religion, thought, belief, opinion, expression, and peaceful assembly, as well as others, in terms which are not in conflict with the statutory expectations, but which may be in conflict with the Catholic school district or Catholic school policies, the court may well find in favor of the student. Indeed, the court could state that such is consistent not only with the Charter but also the Catholic Church's own rights to freedom of conscience and religion extending to them.

The argument in contract appears too weak to seriously consider as "prescribed by law" under section one as students are not normally of the age to give valid consent to enter into a contract and in any event Charter rights are not negotiable.

The implications of the above are important for Catholic schools in Ontario, Alberta, and Saskatchewan as the scope of freedom for non-Catholic students regarding the disregard of denominational norms may be wide indeed.

CHAPTER FIVE

THE FIFTH DIMENSION OF INCLUSION: RACIAL

Race is the fifth dimension of inclusion. This is not a topic normally raised in Canadian Catholic schools in relation to non-Catholic students. This is in counterpoint to the United States where O'Keefe (1997) states,

> In June 1992, members of the Black Clergy Caucus wrote, "Catholic social teachings have been bold and uncompromising." The sad problem, it added, is that these teachings "are all too often unknown, un-preached, un-taught, and un-believed" (Gibson, 1996, p. 8). Even when they are known, preached, taught and believed they most often are not acted upon, with one clear exception: inner-city Catholic schools. Tentative analysis of the Urban Catholic School Study indicates that most non-Catholic students in these schools are African American. Thus, *religious diversity in the schools enhances racial justice.* In light of our history of outright discrimination or complicit silence in the face of such behavior, Catholics in the United States must be committed to the welfare of African Americans. (p. 10) [emphasis added]

Race, although not ostensibly connected to inclusion in Canada, is an issue, unspoken perhaps, but an issue nevertheless. In Saskatchewan's urban centers, there is a substantial First Nations population. Moreover, following the first Gulf War, a significant Islamic population, sponsored by religious groups, immigrated to Canada and settled in Saskatchewan. Anecdotal evidence suggests that Catholic schools with their overt set of religious values and an appreciation for religious matters, have been attractive to that religious minority which in most cases has meant persons of color. Boase (2006) speaks of Ontario's Catholic schools when she says, "Twenty-five per cent of Hamilton's Muslim families send their children to Catholic schools. Other non-Christian students also say they benefit from the system's faith-centred curriculum." As one Islamic student said with respect to the Catholic school in Hamilton, Ontario which she attended, "The way that they teach, they're stricter in the Catholic school . . . There's more homework, more tests and they encourage us to do well in school. It's like they are preparing us for our lives" (Boase, 2006). The sister of that student commented upon the life in the Catholic school saying that they accepted the mandatory religion classes and attendance at school Masses, "We listen . . . [i]t's mostly about God and how to obey Him and that's good to know . . . What's beautiful about the Catholic school . . . is that they accept you. They don't care what religion you are" (Boase, 2006). Indeed, in Canada – where in some schools it appears that 32 % of students are not Catholic – the openness to other religions can engender conversion of some students to other than the Catholic Faith (Green, 2009).

As a researcher I experienced the significance of students of color who were also members of the Islamic religion. In Study #1, a Catholic school principal was reluctant to allow my study of the impact of inclusion upon Catholic high school students as he felt that to do so might make the Muslim students feel excluded from what he saw as a school activity. Moreover, he stated that he did not want to "offend the Muslim families" as the study could be perceived as a "White" study. In the end, he acquiesced to the study being conducted in his school but his reluctance and sensitivity to a matter of race, as well as religion, marks race as a dimension of inclusion, even in a relatively small Western Canadian city.

In Saskatchewan, my research led me in Study #1 to a Catholic high school with a significant number of First Nations students. This number was not a surprise as in Saskatchewan, First Nations are a very large percentage of the province's population. In that school there was no connection between inclusion and race although many First Nations students were not Catholic. I am unable to explain why there is an apparent lack of connection between First Nations students and inclusion whereas there is an ostensible connection between Islamic students and inclusion. The issue of race and inclusion in Canadian Catholic schools is an area in which further studies could be conducted perhaps with the same general quantitative instruments used by Greeley (2002) in his text, "Catholic High Schools and Minority Students."

CHAPTER SIX

THE SIXTH DIMENSION OF INCLUSION: ADMINISTRATION

The sixth dimension of inclusion is administrative in nature as it is concerned with the practical realities of inclusion which face Catholic school administrators which coexist with their pastoral duties to those under their care.

This Chapter draws on several sources of data, Church documents, academic writings, and relies heavily upon this researcher's Study #2 which involved Catholic school administrators in a Western Canadian province, the conceptual framework for which was presented in the Introduction to this book.

The Chapter begins with some Preliminary Considerations and then moves to examine three areas: a) administrative expectations, b) significance of the Entrance Interview, and c) the on-going relationship between the admitted non-Catholic student and the school administration (Donlevy, 2009).

PRELIMINARY CONSIDERATIONS

There are times when a Catholic school principal has a request for admission from both a Catholic student and a non-Catholic student yet there is limited space available within the school. The initial question for the school administrator is whether a non-Catholic student may be selected for admission before the Catholic student. In that respect legislation is important, in Ontario, Alberta, and Saskatchewan, as its wording may place both students on a level playing filed for admission. Moreover, Hawker (1987), albeit within the American context, suggests that matters which are "parochial, academic, financial, attitudinal, and sociological" (p. 8) should be considered when a school administrator is faced with the choice of admitting a Catholic students or a non-Catholic student. In the parochial sphere applications from members of the local parish should have priority in consideration. Academically, if both applicants were equally strong the Catholic student would have priority, yet,

> [The] Catholic [student] . . . must be able to fulfill the academic standards of the school. If the Catholic could not do so and a non-Catholic could, then the non-Catholic might be selected provided he/she manifests a responsible attitude in relation to the purpose and goals of the school. (p. 9)

Hawker (1987) mentions that financially, where a Catholic applicant cannot afford tuition, such is unfortunate but that a non-Catholic applicant may be selected in his or her place. He further suggests that attitudinally,

> Those who attend the Catholic school must be willing to accept its purpose and goals. If Catholic applicants are not willing to do so they should not be accepted. On the other hand, if non-Catholic applicants are willing to accept the purpose and goals, as well as the other criteria for admission, they should be accepted (p. 9).

Lastly, Hawker suggests that in inner-city settings there is a valuable service to be performed by Catholic schools in opening their doors to "non-Catholic blacks and other minorities" (p. 9).

The reader will notice from the above that although Hawker's comments may have some resonance with Canadians, the situation in Canada's constitutionally protected Catholic schools in Ontario, Alberta, and Saskatchewan is distinctly different from the private Catholic schools in the United States of America.

ADMINISTRATIVE EXPECTATIONS

Beyond the preliminary considerations, this researcher's Study #2 was conducted within one Western Canadian Catholic school district's jurisdiction. That Study revealed the following issues with respect to inclusion and Catholic school administration: a) administrative expectations, b) significance of the Entrance Interview, and c) the on-going relationship between the admitted non-Catholic student and the school administration.

Whatever the historical and local cultural idiosyncrasies of the schools, the maintenance of the Catholicity of the schools was seen by all participants as central to their administrative mission. This theme will address the administrative expectations of the participants within three categories: the ethos of the Catholic school in relation to the non-Catholic students' behavior, the importance of the non-Catholic family's faith commitment, and the administrators' sense of the importance of inclusion.

Catholic Ethos of the School and Non-Catholic Students' Behavior

Although normal administrative concerns respecting the admission of students, such as classroom space and the availability of special services for students with special needs were considered important, it was the participants' deep commitment to and understanding of the necessity of maintaining the school's distinctly Catholic identity and the religious ethos of the same that were predominant in their interviews with the researcher. All participants stated that their expectation was that non-Catholic students would overtly display respect for the schools' religious traditions, religious curriculum, and liturgies. One participant stated:

> If we are to offer a Catholic school system, then there should be a strong Catholic aspect to it. If we don't have our faith, then really we're not different from the school across the street that offers . . . public education. So if there isn't a difference in our faith involvement, then there is no purpose

> for us to be in existence . . . If people don't want to buy into that then they don't have to come here – that is our expectation (Study #2).

A second participant said:

> I don't see how you can fully be a member of the school community without participating . . . [in the] Mass . . . and those type of faith practices . . . and being reverent . . . [it] is not an option (Study #2).

Importance of the Non-Catholic Family's Faith Commitment

All of the school administrators perceived their school as a community which included the families of all students. Moreover, the importance of those families' faith commitment was seen as very important for students and the school. One administrator said,

> Part of what we are doing is trying to build a community . . . family and school . . . if the family does not have that legacy of having any kind of faith environment at home, the moment it's a struggle, the moment the student comes home and says oh I don't like that . . . well, they don't participate. They have never . . . been practiced in building community and being part of a faith community. . . If they don't have enough history, a practice of faith, I think they struggle with all the things that we try to build as a community (Study #2).

A second stated,

> I think it is important . . . it makes it a lot easier for students to come into a faith filled environment if they're bringing their own faith foundation with them. . . . it makes it a lot easier for them to understand our teachings, to understand our way of proceeding. Having said that, the key determining [factor] is an openness (Study #2).

A third said,

> I think [the non-Catholic family's faith commitment] it is pretty significant. If the parent is thinking that the child is going to pick-up some sort of faith just by going to school and not getting any help with it at home or reinforcement with it at home, then what is it going to mean to the child? . . . If there are no fundamental . . . beliefs at home . . . there's no way that these things that we've been discussing at school are going to sink in (Study #2).

Lastly, one administrator noted that,

> When we have assemblies, say a band concert or something like that, we open and close with prayers and we just expect that they will be part of what we do. When we have school council meetings for the parent council we start with a prayer. They need to . . . be accepting of it but they do not have to participate. Parents do not have to attend Masses, they just have to accept that

> we will be [holding Masses in the school] and that that is part of our [school] culture (Study #2).

The Administrators' Sense of the Importance of Inclusion

All school administrators' expectations included the idea that inclusion was a positive aspect of Catholic education. The idea expressed was that it contributed the vibrancy of the school community, injected a sense of religion into student's lives, which they could choose to accept, and was part of the sacred task of the school as a Catholic institution. Moreover, it ameliorated the possibility of a ghetto mentality developing within the school. As one administrator said,

> I have a sense of what makes a vibrant Catholic school . . . and I don't think that I would want the Catholic percentage to drop below seventy percent. Having said that, I don't think I'd really . . . want to see the [Catholic student percentage] rise much higher than eighty [percent]. You know that 20 to 30 percent of non-Catholic students give us a diversity that is a great challenge in our school. I don't mean a challenge to meet; it is a challenge for us . . . not to be too focused on our own way of proceeding and thereby become closed minded to other practices and people (Study #2).

A second administrator stated,

> A lot of times I figure, well, maybe if we can at least give this child some sort of taste of what religion is like . . . we may have a little success with them in their life . . . We are an evangelizing school board. We . . . proclaim the Word of God. I don't think it's a goal for us to convert them [non-Catholic students] . . . If they realize that God is in their lives and they feel that this is important to them, then that is just a bonus (Study #2).

SIGNIFICANCE OF THE ENTRANCE INTERVIEW

The entrance interview of the non-Catholic parents and their child with the Catholic school principal is the threshold moment for the inclusion of non-Catholic students. Hawker (1987) suggests that five points should be covered during that conversation:

- The Catholic school participates in the evangelical and educational mission of the Church.
- All parents should understand and accept the purpose, goals, and objectives of the Catholic school.
- All students who attend the Catholic school are expected to participate in religion class.
- All non-Catholic students who attend the Catholic school should be encouraged to participate in the liturgical and para-liturgical programs within the school to the extent that they are able.

– All students who attend the Catholic school are expected to participate in programs of service that are sponsored by the school. (p. 30)

He also makes clear that "during the interview . . . parents should be assisted to understand that the Catholic school participates in the educational and evangelizing mission of the Church" (p. 29). Five years before his writing of 1987 was published, Hawker wrote an article in a Catholic journal, Momentum, which clarified the distinction between, and the synthesis of, evangelization and the role of the catechist. He said,

> The catechist is not concerned with proselytization, which implies a coercion to become a Catholic. The task of the evangelizing catechist is to offer an option to the students. Like Christ, he or she shares the Good News with those who do not know it. Although that option is invaluable from the catechist's perspective, it is simply one option among a number available to the students. Some students may not choose to respond by making a religious commitment. Others may decide to accept Christ and his message as interpreted by the Catholic tradition. Another group may commit themselves to a Protestant understanding of Christ and his teachings. Whatever the response or lack thereof of the catechist must always respect the right of the student to exercise freedom of conscience. (Hawker, 1982, p. 28)

Essentially he makes the point that there is no separation between evangelization and catechesis which was clarified by John Paul II (1979) "Let us first of all recall that there is no separation or opposition between catechesis and evangelization. Nor can the two be simply identified with each other. Instead, they have close links whereby they integrate and complement each other" (para 18).

In Study #2 the entrance interview was a focus of attention as it was crucial in determining whether the child would be admitted to the school. In that respect, the interview covered four general categories: the interview form, the clarification of the school's expectations of the parents and potential student, the giving of fair notice to parents of the consequences of breach of the agreement, and seeking to understand the non-Catholic family's openness to the expectations of the Catholic school as well as the extent of the non-Catholic family's commitment to its own faith.

The Interview Entrance Form

All participants agreed that the admission of the non-Catholic student, beyond the standard generic administrative issues of the student's academic record, available space, and special programs if the student had particular physical or mental challenges, was dependant upon the nature of the initial interview with the student and her or his parents.

The entrance interview normally lasted 20 to 30 minutes and followed the general outline of a series of generic questions in the Interview Entrance Form (Appendix E).

In general, the purpose of the form seems to be to focus the attention of the administrator on certain relevant topics and in particular to inform the non-Catholic family of the school's behavioral expectations of their child, including that the parents would be expected to accept the enforcement of the behavioral norms should such be necessary.

The interview form states, "We are overt in our Faith and it permeates all that we do" and asks "Do you have any concerns with your child being exposed to the teachings of the church and the teachings of the gospel?" "Would those teachings be in any way contradictory to your religious denomination?" It further asks, "Do you have objections to your child participating in prayer, the rosary religious celebrations, liturgies and masses, Ash Wednesday Celebration," and "respecting the values and practices of our faith?"

One wonders how non-Catholic parents could reasonably respond to the above questions in a twenty minute interview without any knowledge of the Catholic Faith. Presumably, the school administrator would verbally fill in the gaps and explain the relevant Catholic values and practices including providing examples of what an acceptable level of "participation" looked like within the school. The final few lines of the interview document state "Please sign below that we have had an interview."

The questions on the form appear weak in not focusing the non-Catholic parents and students upon the existential rather than merely the behavioral expectations of the school administration. What appears to be missing is a clearly written statement to be read by all non-Catholic families respecting the expected evolutionary and experiential nature of their child's faith journey while attending the Catholic school. Further, there is no commentary respecting the assistance which the non-Catholic parents would be expected to provide to their child in that regard.

The interview form appears disorganized as it moves from generic administrative issues to denominational matters and then back to the former. If the form was in five parts that would arguably be a more organized approach to the entrance interview: a) generic administrative matters, b) an explanation of Catholic values and practices within the school, c) specific questions to parents related to those values and practices, d) a commitment from the parents to the support of the school administration for their child's behavioral acquiescence to those values and practices, and e) a persuasively binding statement from the parents to their commitments prior to their signature on the form. It might also be prudent for the school administrator to have a personal list of specific values and practices which could be raised at each interview. For example, that although the Catholic Faith views the Bible with great respect, it is only one part of the triumvirate of sources which constitute the sources of the interpretation of the values and norms of the Catholic Church. The Holy Scriptures, along with the Tradition of the Faith and the living Magisterium (Bainvel, 1912) of the Catholic Church form the tripartite source for its values and practices which is not the case in other religions. Indeed, it can be argued that the Catholic Church invokes "the authority of the natural law, the Scriptures and the Tradition, the ordinary and universal Magisterium, the disciplinary tradition of the Church, the unanimous agreement of the bishops [and] the authority which Christ conferred upon Peter and his successors" (Fisher, 2007).

This point was raised by one school administrator who related a comment made by a non-Catholic parent to him, "You say you're Catholic but how come you're not Christian?" The school administrator understood that question to mean "[the non-Catholic parents'] interpretation of [being] Christian is that you take the Bible as a literary source."

Clarification of the School's Expectations of the Parents and Potential Student

During the interview, administrators looked to the openness, if not a commitment, of the student and parents to a sense of religion as an important element in their lives. This was consistent with the administrators' expectations and provided an opportunity for the school administrator to explain the Catholic school's religious culture, the behavioral expectations of students, the important elements of the on-going faith journey of the student and the necessity of parental support for their child's journey and the school's religious mission. A school administrator said,

> They say . . . 'We want our child exposed to some religion.' And I say to them are they exposed to [religion] now? Most of the answers I get are 'No, we want them to make up their own mind.' I say to them . . . is it not difficult for them to make up their own mind if you're not exposing them to this at home? . . . I say, if your child is in trouble with math, are you going to help them with math? And they say yes. And I say, if your child is having trouble with religion, how are you going to help them with religion (Study #2)?

A second stated,

> The process we have gone through is to sit down with the parent and the student and to interview, talk, describe to them what our culture is about, share with them the dynamics of being in a Catholic school and determine at that interview whether that's something they want to be part of. Whether they can join in respectfully or do they have any issues that would cause conflict . . . daily prayer . . . speaking about Jesus . . . (Study #2).

A third reiterated the above,

> In that meeting . . . when you're talking about the morning prayer . . . I say . . . all I'm going to ask Betty [a hypothetical student] to do is, when everyone else is praying – you're going to make it look like you're in prayer . . . and they make that commitment (Study #2).

It was openness to the experience of faith within the Catholic school which was seen as the predictor of the non-Catholic student's success, enjoyment, and her or his acceptance of the Catholic prayer community's milieu in which she or he was entering. It was also made clear that conformity to the goals of the school in a religious sense would be on-going over the term of attendance from year to year if the student was admitted. In the event that in the future remediation of a student's behavior at school in relation to behavioral conformity was required the parents were told that they would be involved in ameliorating the concern and expected to support the school administration.

A third administrator stated a rather strong position which will be referred to and qualified later in this paper,

> I say to the potential new enrollments and the families that we expect all of our kids to make the sign of the cross. If you don't know the Our Father we expect you to learn the Our Father. If you don't know the Hail Mary, we expect you to learn the Hail Mary . . . I say to the child, do you think that would be a challenge for you or . . . something that you think you could embrace (Study #2)?

The above injunction was based upon the administrator's belief that "[It is] absolutely critical to make sure that we have kind of a homogeneous approach to the prayer life of our school (Study #2)." The administrator went on to say:

> It comes down to letting them know here is everything we stand for; here's what you can expect. You need to make sure that you're comfortable with that, and if you are not, this is probably not the school for you (Study #2).

Giving of Fair Notice to Parents of the Consequences of Breach

School administrators noted that while some non-Catholic parents were quite willing to agree to whatever was required in order to have their child admitted to the Catholic school. Such acquiescence disappeared later should difficulties arise between their child and the school administration or when the religious expectations of the non-Catholic parents were not met by the Catholic school administrator.

One participant stated:

> I'm very, very forthright with parents. I say that there are a couple of different aspects I have to look at; one is whether or not the parent is going to be open to the fact that we have faith in our school. And quite honestly, over the years I've found that people are really, really willing to lie about that. A lot of people will say 'Oh no. The faith is an important aspect; that's why we wanted your school.' Later on when they are accepted, as it turns out faith means absolutely nothing, they don't really care. They have learned that's one of the things we look for . . . [In one case] I let their child into the school and then they came to me after the fact and said we don't have our child attending any of your religion classes and we don't want them participating in prayer (Study #2).

In contradistinction to the above position another administrator said,

> The child has to partake in learning prayer, at least to the point of showing some sort of respect for that. We don't require that they make the sign of the cross or . . . say the Hail Mary . . . but we do expect them to stand, be quiet

> during that time while the other kids are doing it. We do expect all our children to go to our Masses and our celebrations and we also encourage them to go up during communion and to receive a blessing instead of the communion itself (Study #2).

> The direction from the District is that . . . you cannot force people to make the sign of the cross, and if the student is a conscientious objector, so that they have dealt with this on some kind of conscious level, we involve the parents in the . . . discussion, and the student, and then . . . I necessarily have to relive them of the obligation to make the sign of the cross. But they are going to be respectful and they are going to do what everybody else is doing. They are going to stand when everyone else is standing, sit when everybody else is sitting, and at least physically then you know, continue that (Study #2).

To reiterate, it is fair to say that beyond the normal administrative expectations of the school administrator, the participants seemed focused upon the importance of the religious nature of the school district's mission and in particular sought to ensure that the religious ethos of her or his Catholic school was not upset by the admission of non-Catholic students who would disabuse the opportunity to be part of the school as a faith community. As one administrator stated, "I probe the question a little bit to find out mostly are they going to be [act] contrary to our faith? Is our faith going to be something that will cause difficulty for them or for us?"

The non-Catholic family's openness to the expectations of the Catholic school as well as the extent of the non-Catholic family's commitment to its own faith When a non-Catholic family is strongly committed to their faith, and understands or at least respects the religious norms of the Catholic Faith, this usually is a good indicator of their child's success in adapting to the ethos of the Catholic school.

> We will have non-Catholics who are very devout in their own faith and that's why they want the Catholic school because . . . it's a faith aspect [to them]. Often times our non-Catholic are a really, really positive [part of the school community] . . . because they are very devout in their own faiths . . . the children are very devout in their faith and they're very good and positive influences in terms of Christianity (Study #2).

In response to the question, "How important is it that those parents are committed to their own faith?" one school administrator stated, "in my view it is very important . . . If I get the sense that . . . they're coming to the school number one because of it being a faith environment then it's usually going to be a good situation (Study #2)."

Following that first part of the interview, the school administrators appeared to go through a process of discernment respecting the impact of religion and faith upon the non-Catholic parents, their willingness to support the administration in ensuring the compliance of their child with the religious norms of the school, and to support the administration in that regard, as well as the potential for a latent resentment to those norms on the part of the student and/or the parents. Based upon that assessment the administrator either admitted or rejected the non-Catholic student's application for admission to the school.

It is important to note that although the interview form is not used to screen the entry of Catholic families who seek admission for their children to the Catholic school; that fact does not argue against seeking the same understandings of the Catholic family. If anything, it argues for the same process to be applied to Catholic families as well as non-Catholic families. Although Catholic schools within the participants' school district are required to accept Catholic students, as the district defines that term, a searching interview involving those applicants would be useful but administratively prohibitive due to the expenditure of time.

Lastly, this chapter would be remiss if it did not point out that a major missing piece of this research is the admission of non-Christian students, for example, those of the Islamic Faith. One such study exists but more are required (Burwell, 2005). That research might well cause the findings of this research to be greatly revised vis-à-vis such non-Catholic families – particularly in light of the Catholic Church's undertaking, as aforementioned, to provide freedom of conscience and religion to non-Catholics within the Catholic school.

THE ON-GOING RELATIONSHIP

Beyond the entrance interview, the on-going relationship with the non-Catholic student was discussed by each participant. Two categories emerged from those discussions: no special programming and an invitation to non-Catholic students to express their faith beliefs through participation in the school's liturgical celebrations.

No Special Programming

It is fair to say that the Catholic school administrators in this study did not see the need for any special programs within their schools for non-Catholic students. One administrator was perhaps a bit harsh in stating,

> We don't do anything special for our non-Catholic students. Do I think we should? No, I do not think we should. We are a Catholic school . . . I don't see changing my school or my programs to meet the needs of other religions . . . This is a Catholic school and we service the needs of Catholic students (Study #2).

However, that same administrator later stated that if a non-Catholic student group wanted to hold Bible reading sessions, "I wouldn't have a problem with something like that (Study #2)".

Invitation to students. All participants well understood the benefits which accrued to their schools as a result of inclusion. In particular, the benefits when non-Catholic students took upon themselves the opportunity to become involved in the school's public moments of faith and in school leadership roles. One administrator said,

> Some of the students who are non-Catholic are in a Christian rock band so they sing along with us at church . . . they are part of the ministry. . . the idea is that we are all on a [faith] journey (Study #2).

One participant noted:

> We definitely have a very active non-Catholic Christian population . . . They're leaders in student council; they're part of prayer groups . . . When we have retreats . . . the kids are active . . . in services . . . mass or liturgy of the school, quite often non-Catholics would be in leadership roles (Study #2).

Moreover, in one school a non-Catholic youth group leader from outside of the school was welcomed into a school – conditionally. One school administrator stated,

> I did sit down with him one day and say listen, I like having you here because the kids like you (and he is only promoting God and Christ and Christianity in general terms), but I said that it can never be perceived that you are actually promoting your faith or trying to recruit . . . we . . . wouldn't allow that (Study #2).

It is also the case that at least in one school there is a "student prayer group "facilitated by . . . teachers . . . [which] is inclusive of all faiths. . . it is [composed of] predominantly Protestant students (Study #2)."

It is suggested by this researcher that an Assisi Day (Benedict XVI, 2006) as a time for inter-religious prayer could be held, on rare occasions, in Catholic schools where various faith traditions could meet for the purpose of prayer. This would not be to encourage syncretism or religious relativism but rather to provide, as have Popes John Paul II and Benedict XVI, an opportunity to display unity in reverence for life and respect for all no matter their faith beliefs. It is recognized that when dealing with adolescents their ability to distinguish between inter-religious prayer and prayer and syncretism may be difficult but such is part of the price to be paid for inclusion and the respect for all religions which accompany that decision. It may be that, arguably, the real difficulty would be whether the distinction could be made by the Catholic teachers in the school (Donlevy, 2003a).

POINTS OF CONFRONTATION

Seven points of confrontation were mentioned by the school administrators in this study. The first three points are common in most schools and do not go to the nature of the Catholic school per se: drug usage, disrespectful use of clothing, and instances of adolescent rebellion against school authority. However, four other matters were deemed significant to the Catholic school per se, not because Catholic students did not also evidence the same in kind, but rather that the administrative approaches to those concerns were different in quality than for Catholic students: refusal to participate in specifically religious matters, overt disrespect for the Catholic faith – its beliefs and practices – in classes, sexual promiscuity, and abortion. It is to the latter four matters in relation to non-Catholic students and their remediation through the Catholic school administration that I now turn after a description of a fundamental divide within the understandings of certain Catholic school administrators in this study.

A Fundamental Divide

It is fair to say that there is a division in the understanding of this study's participating Catholic school administrators with respect to their jurisdiction after school hours in so far as non-conforming moral behavior is concerned. The first position is voiced in the following quotation from a school administrator when commenting upon two non-Catholic students who choose to live in a common law relationship:

> Once they are off campus, I don't see myself as the moral police . . . There is no contract for an 18 year old or 17 year old to say [to them] that just because they come to a Catholic school . . . they have to lead a Catholic moral life outside of it . . . I'm not sure that I would sit in judgment . . . Two people . . . students 17-18 moving in together – while I would not recommend it – and I would help [and] work with the family . . . [to] see other choices, [but] basically out of the school land when they're sixteen – they can sign into my school . . . [Moreover] once they are admitted to my school, once they're registered and are of my school . . . and they [then] move out of their houses and they're sixteen, it's not my call (Study #2).

On the other hand, another school administrator stated,

> We know that they [Catholic and non-Catholic students] have a lot of partying on the weekends, perhaps a number of sexual partners . . . parents are concerned, teachers are concerned . . . everyone knows what's going on and knows . . . [when] we have a child in crisis. We've definitely brought the parents into the picture . . . I'm very blunt with parents and say *you know it is none of my business and its only my opinion*, but here's what needs to happen for the sake of the child. I had one [student] last year who had moved out of home and wasn't officially living with her boyfriend, but in reality was. Her health was terrible and . . . I just had an open and frank conversation with her parents as I could [emphasis added] (Study #2).

A third school administrator was more definitive then the last participant, stating, "I would have to ask them to leave the school (Study #2)."

The difference between the three positions is startling. Whereas the first saw the issue in jurisdictional terms outside of school hours, the second viewed the issue in terms of a pastoral duty owed to each student in crisis, a duty which exists because the student is part of the Catholic school community. This second view seems to intuitively take into account the existence of every school's student sub-culture and the effect of what is considered by the Catholic Church as immoral behavior on a student's peers and the community's sense of morality. Indeed, for the administration to fail to act might well be seen as willful blindness or a lack of moral certainty on the issue. The third administrator approached the issue with a "matter of fact" attitude which seemed to not consider the complexities expressed by the first and second participants.

Refusal to Participate in Religious Matters

Having been admitted to a Catholic school, a very, very small minority of non-Catholic students determined that they no longer wish to participate in religious activities. That decision followed by a refusal to participate was seen by the Catholic school administrators to warrant an administrative response. One administrator said to students, "You know this is what you decided to join, nobody forced you to come here, this is what we're about, now you need to be at least respectful (Study #2)."

Disrespect for the Catholic Faith

Other non-Catholic students chose to vocalize their disdain for the Catholic Church's religious beliefs and moral norms in classes. It is worthwhile and important to note that this disdain for Catholic beliefs was very rare and not at all the norm for non-Catholic students. There is some evidence from other research that it is a much more common phenomenon amongst Catholic high school students than non-Catholic students in a Catholic school. Evidence suggests that non-Catholic students are much more respectful of Catholic beliefs that a third of a school's student body who are un-churched Catholic students (Donlevy, 2003a).

With respect to a non-Catholic student receiving the Eucharist one participant said,

> I think I've had non-Catholic students who received the Eucharist . . . rather than choose a blessing. I . . . try to discern . . . what's the motive for the action? . . . It's really an education issue with the student . . . it can become an educational moment . . . If it became a public event I would pursue discipline (Study #2).

The above comment is consistent with an approach to religious challenges facing individuals on their personal faith journeys while working within Catholic schools. Administrators tend to apply a pastoral approach to those issues unless the challenge to the norms of the Catholic Faith are public and thus attract scandal to the Faith and deleteriously affect the ethos of the Catholic school.

Sexual Promiscuity

High school students involved in sexual promiscuity is, of course, not confined to non-Catholic students and knows no religious boundaries. Fraught with sexually transmitted disease, teen pregnancy, behavioral disorders, depression, and eating disorders, sexual promiscuity is arguably fed by media advertising, peer pressure, and a desire for instant gratification without responsibility.

In the case of a student identified by the Catholic school administrators to be at risk, all administrators agreed that parents and the school councilor are called-in to assist in the student's remediation. In the case of a non-Catholic student, one Catholic school administrator suggested that the assistance of a non-Catholic minister, when suggested by non-Catholic parents, would be asked for to assist in the amelioration of the errant student's behavior. It appears that amongst some of the Catholic administrators there was an understanding of the importance of including non-Catholic religious support for non-Catholic students who may be in crisis. Although this was not a unanimous suggestion by the participants, when it was raised by the researcher it was responded to positively. Surprisingly, only one participant suggested that the local Catholic priest would be consulted in such circumstances with Catholic students. That was the only instance in the research when the involvement of a Catholic priest was mentioned.

In general, the following comment summarized the participants' position with respect to students living in a common-law relationship,

> If kids become sexually active, if kids are involved in any kind of . . . self destructive behavior, we're going to minister to those kids as best we can and bring them to the face of Jesus . . . I would expect staff advisors to let them know that it's [a common law relationship] a poor life decision . . . [staff advisors] would involve themselves in . . . discussion with the [student's] parents (Study #2).

Abortion. The issue of teen abortion is not new to Catholic school administrators. One participant related that a school counselor "got a phone call [from a non-Catholic student] . . . saying she was . . . . [having] an abortion in the next ten minutes . . . (Study #2)."

One participant was clear that these matters were normally handled in confidence by the school counselor whereas another school administrator believed that it was of such importance that the school administration should be involved from the student's revelation. One administrator said, "Well, I haven't addressed the situation because it is confidential and I shouldn't have known about it . . . I haven't approached the abortion issue at all . . . I think it's just now about the child and not the act (Study #2)."

Another participant took another position stating that in such a case,

> The school councilor would be in contact with me so that I was looped on what was going on, but it would not become general knowledge. We would for sure work with the parents and the child to encourage a full-term pregnancy and adoption. But beyond that, *if the . . . parents and the child decide otherwise, then we would support them through the process* to make

> sure that the kid, that the young mother, the young child is as well taken care of as possible [emphasis added] (Study #2).

In both of the above cases there are obviously administrative and religious concerns. Clearly, given the nature of Catholic education, the possibility of a student, Catholic or non-Catholic, having an abortion is of the gravest concern. First, such matters are of the utmost importance to the school administrator as the spiritual leader of the Catholic school. Second, it is problematic that a Catholic school administration would support a student's decision to procure an abortion – except in the most egregious student health situation and then only after consultation with the local Catholic priest.

CONCLUSION

This Chapter has offered that, with regard to Study #2, the Catholic school administrators interviewed perceived four major themes with respect to the inclusion of non-Catholic students in their schools: a) the school administrators' expectations, b) the significance of the preliminary interview, c) the ongoing relationship of the non-Catholic student to the Catholic school, and d) points of confrontation with the Catholic school administration. Categories under each major theme suggested that the participants were concerned with the schools' Catholic identity, the behavioral conformity of non-Catholic students to the schools' Catholic ethos, and support from non-Catholic students' parents when that conformity was lacking. Moreover, the importance of the non-Catholic family's commitment to its own faith was considered important to the success of the on-going relationship of the non-Catholic student and the Catholic school.

In matters of breach of that conformity by a non-Catholic student, the participants, although not unanimous, generally understood that a pastoral approach was best employed in seeking remediation of the non-Catholic student's non-conforming behavior. That remediation could include, in some cases, the involvement of a non-Catholic religious minister. Issues of non-conformity in the areas of refusal to participate in religious matters, disrespect for the Catholic Faith, sexual promiscuity, and abortion, although present with non-Catholic students, was treated differently by administrators when those matters involved Catholic students arguably because, where applicable, the arguments with respect to such behavior could differ between the Catholic Faith and non-Catholic faiths. There was a fundamental disagreement amongst the participants' regarding their Catholic school administrator's jurisdiction on matters of the moral behavior of students after school hours.

If this Study indicates that there is concern in several Catholic high schools regarding the treatment of non-Catholic students, it may reflect the same concern n other school jurisdictions (Grajczonek, Ryan, Chambers, 2007).

CHAPTER SEVEN

THE SEVENTH DIMENSION OF INCLUSION: PEDAGOGICAL

The seventh dimension is pedagogical in nature. It is incumbent upon both Catholic school administrators and teachers to be sensitive to the non-Catholic student's sense of being the "Other" among the Catholic student body. The general meaning of the term the "Other" refers to "another person, tradition, history, ancestors, being, etc." (Schwandt, 2007, p. 213). However, with the understanding that to truly encounter the Other, rather than merely receive a reflected vision of what one already believes exists as another person, what is required is not analysis of an alleged objective truth or thing or person but rather dialogue and conversation and being prepared for the encounter as one being to another being rather than to a thing or object constitutes "the conditions under which understanding emerges" (p. 214). Certainly the continental philosophical understanding of the Other is complex (Lacan, 1964; Levinas, 1972; Buber, 2002).

For the purposes of this book, the significance of the meaning of that term for understanding the non-Catholic in Catholic schools is a recognition by the Catholic students and teachers of the non-Catholic student as the Other within their school which, in part, allows the Catholic student and teachers to identify and define themselves. It may be said, as if I was a teacher in the Catholic school, that the non-Catholic student is beyond my "horizon of intelligibility," yet I learn about myself because of the Other's presence. This is surely true as Catholic students have experienced this phenomenon when in class with non-Catholic students (Study #1). As one Catholic students said,

> It's good to have someone to challenge our faith, and to have someone to help make us stronger, if everyone was just Catholic, it would just be the same thing . . . Making us think about our faith is a good thing. . . It's shocking if you've been raised since you were a kid and its like, as if [you] were three and somebody said there is no Santa, and you're like, "What?" It's the same as how you'd feel at that point . . . It's shocking in a few ways. For one, you may be questioning yourself, because you're thinking like, "Oh! Maybe not everyone believes what I believe!" And there's definitely a conflict. And you wonder if people aren't on the right track maybe, and it's disturbing (Study #1).

Another Catholic student related,

> I was actually pleasantly surprised yesterday in particular at our Reconciliation [Celebration]. I was sitting around and several people I know who are non-Catholics [were there] but I didn't feel distracted whatsoever and I felt that

> they were paying the utmost respect with what was going on . . . Yesterday, I especially felt like Wow! This is really nice to have this whole group of people even though we might not share the faith in religion we're all doing this as a community. Yeah. I was really pleasantly surprised by the behavior of everybody as a whole. (Study #1; Donlevy, 2006b)

At the same time, non-Catholic students have encountered Catholic students and Catholic teachers as their Other and have similarly been changed as the following quotation from Study #3 evidences.

> Catholic high school helped me discover who I was. It helped m – like kind of being all by myself [as a non-Catholic in a classroom] it helped me deepen my strength and it helped me deepen my relationship with Christ and it helped me ask those questions that I'd never asked before but I wanted to ask . . . It really helped me to strengthen my relationship with Christ.

Catholic teachers have also experienced non-Catholic students as the Other and as a result the teachers themselves have been changed. These are the statements of two Catholic high school teachers:

> Sometimes I wonder how welcome non-Catholic students feel. I've never felt a sense or feeling of [their] not being welcome. That question of "I am not Catholic and therefore he [the teacher] sees me as a second-class citizen" . . . I don't think they feel that way, but I can see where that might happen (Study #1).

> I have been on the receiving end of it [prayer] as well. I've got a couple of car accidents under my belt, and knowing that my kids . . . [said] many prayers . . . For me [many] by non-Catholics . . . it's just comforting . . . At that particular time, it really didn't matter if they were of [my] faith (Study #1).

The issue of encountering the Other in reciprocity and the nature of that relationship as viewed by continental philosophy with the hope that such would enrich the pedagogy of the Other would be very helpful to understanding the inclusion of non-Catholic students within Catholic schools. That topic requires a deeper consideration from the lens of continental philosophy and phenomenological inquiry which are beyond the scope of this book.

On a practical basis, pedagogically there is arguably a necessity that Catholic teachers recognize and value the individual student, Catholic or non-Catholic, notwithstanding disagreement and at times discord in the class due to differing opinions on belief and faith within classes. This means maintaining a balance between an appreciation and respect for "difference" yet pursuing the "evangelization" of the Catholic youth within the Catholic school community thorough the clear centrality of the Catholic message. Not an easy task to achieve, not an easy balance to maintain. Moreover, as noted under the Legal Dimension, the overriding respect for the non-Catholic student's right to freedom of conscience is paramount and hence she or he is not to be evangelized by those in the Catholic school.

The issue of whether or not a non-Catholic student should be compelled to attend a school's religion classes, liturgies, the Mass, and the Sacrament of Reconciliation seems settled at least amongst the school administrators which this researcher has encountered.

Essentially, it is arguable that non-Catholic student attendance at school liturgies, Mass, and the Sacrament of Reconciliation are not pedagogical issues, per se. That may be so but the content of the Religion Classes and the experiences within those classes are surely pedagogical issues. With respect to content, Hill (1999) suggests that the alternatives have been, confessional, analytical, and phenomenological.

> The classic case of non-neutral RE is the *confessional* approach which has held centre stage throughout history, and continues to be taken for granted in most non-Western countries. Its intention has been to confirm or produce in the learner allegiance to a particular faith, and its method has tended to be dogmatic instruction. (p.1)

The analytical style "approached religion as an object of sociological study in which the student is encouraged to adopt a posture of scientific detachment and avoid personal engagement" (p.1).

The phenomenological approach was devised to avoid partisanship. Ninian Smart (1968) provided a formal grid of six dimensions through which the phenomenon of "a religious tradition" could be viewed while "bracketing out" the issue of the truth of its belief-claims, and the Birmingham Syllabus reflected this approach in prescribing the study of six major religions (p.1).

Although this author has difficulty with the approach to religious studies offered by Hill, his critique is powerful with respect to curriculum in so far as it relates to religious studies. Catholic schools have the fortunate guidance of the local bishop with respect to the curriculum which will be used within his diocese. Indeed under Canon Law (Code of Canon Law, 1983, Canons # 804, 805, 806) it is the local bishop who is ultimately responsible for religious education within Catholic schools.

At the end of the day it is the Catholic teacher – who she or he is at the core – that is the pedagogical conduit for the Gospel message to the non-Catholic student. The description of the Catholic teacher in Lay Catholics Witnesses to Faith (Congregation, 1982) is appropriate not only for the Catholic students but also the non-Catholic students.

In Study #3, the non-Catholic students found in one Catholic teacher in particular, a willingness to hear and understand their voices and perspectives, while he espoused within the Catholic school the theological singularity of his own faith. His presence gives resonance to the existence of the ideal Catholic school teacher whose presence in the Catholic school is crucial to the school's foundation as a Catholic community (Ford, 1997). All students met the same teacher in their high school and although not all took classes with him, they had nothing but praise for him. The comments of four non-Catholic students from Study #3 follow hereafter.

> He really challenged me . . . he really opened up a lot of doors and a lot of windows and helped me to understand what and why I believed (Study # 3).

> He was awesome! . . . open and he let you discuss things in class. He was just really great! Like, he had his views but he didn't push them on the student which was really good (Study # 3).

> I love him! He was awesome! He is probably one of the most genuine counselors I have ever known . . . he honestly, sincerely cares about students . . . and he seriously loves God and he cares about people. He is just a good guy. He is someone who you could go to and talk to (Study # 3).

The last comment was from one student in Study #3 who remained very angry with his four years in the Catholic high school.

> He's a very good man. He was totally open to everyone's freedom of religion, expression . . . I think he got stuck with a really horrible curriculum. I befriended [the teacher] quite a bit, I mean, he's a really intelligent man and he's really caring. I have no problems with him at all (Study # 3).

All of the students felt that they could go to this teacher due to his friendliness, optimism, lack of hypocrisy, genuineness, candor, and because they believed that he sincerely cared about students. His presence indicates that orthodoxy and orthopraxis are not incommensurable in the Catholic high school. He offered the participants, and presumably all students, the great gift which Buber (2002) speaks of,

> Trust, trust in the world, because this human being exists – that is the most inward achievement of the relation in education. Because this human being exists, meaninglessness, however hard pressed you are by it, cannot be the real truth. Because this human being exists, in the darkness, the light lies hidden, in fear salvation, and in the callousness of one's fellow men the great Love. (p. 116)

Notwithstanding the above, I suggest that there may be some concern with the issue of whether or not a Catholic school should provide opportunities for other than Christian prayer in the school (Caldwell, 2008).

In sum, it appears that the personality and manifest and sincere religious commitment of the teacher in the Catholic high school can have a tremendous effect upon the non-Catholic student. It is of great and lasting import to a student when a teacher displays a strong and sincere conviction regarding the importance and relevance of the ethic of care within the context of the Catholic faith. Indeed, pedagogically, it appears that it is the nature of the relationship which exists between the non-Catholic student as the Other and the Catholic teacher which is central to the pedagogical dimension of inclusion. It seems, therefore, that orthopraxis rather than orthodoxy may be the key to the spiritual nature of the pedagogical relationship.

CHAPTER EIGHT

THE EIGHTH DIMENSION OF INCLUSION: PSYCHOLOGICAL

During the writing of this book, I gave much thought to the various scholarly writers I had read in my undergraduate and graduate years: Kohlberg (1981), Gilligan (1982), Freud (1923), Piaget (1932), Erikson (1950), and Harris (1998). It seemed intuitively correct that an understanding of psychology would be relevant to understanding the phenomenon of non-Catholic students in Catholic schools, not just from the perspective of the non-Catholic student but also the perspective of the Catholic students. As my research progressed, that intuition proved to be correct and further, it was obvious that psychological theory also applied to the impact which inclusion made upon Catholic teachers and Catholic school administrators. One might assume that there may also be a psychological effect or effects upon at least some non-Catholic parents whose children attend Catholic schools – but I have no evidence for that assertion.

As my research continued I found that others had been thinking about the relationship of human psychology and the development of an individual's faith. It is true that the narratives associated with the lives of saints provided stories of faith journeys but recent scholarship attempted to relate such faith journeys to psychological scholarship particularly with regard to psychological stages. James Fowler's (1981) "Stages of Faith: The psychology of human development and the quest for meaning" provided a link between Kohlberg's theory of staged development, based in part I believe upon the conception of staged development suggested in the work of Piaget (1932) and Erickson (1950).

This Chapter deals with the Eighth Dimension and is in three parts: Part I provides the findings on the psychological effects of inclusion upon Catholic students (Donlevy, 2003a, 2006b), Catholic teachers (Donlevy, 2003a, 2007b), and non-Catholic students (Donlevy, 2008a). Part II offers a few brief thoughts on the significance of those findings within the context of the works of Harris (1998), Erickson (1950), Kohlberg (1981), Gilligan (1982), and Noddings (1984). Part III offers a presentation of Fowler's stages as well as an alternative approach; one might say existential approach, to faith development viewed through the writing of James Loder (1998). There are other theories (Osler & Gmünder, 1991, Osler 1991a, 1991b) and revisionary models of Fowler's approach, but for the purposes of this Part the focus will be upon the approaches proffered by Fowler (1981, 1991) and Loder (1998).

PART I

The Catholic Student

It comes as no surprise that most teenagers do not want to belong – to look cool – nor do they wish to see others "left out." To quote a Grade 10 Catholic high school student in Study #1 (all of the quotations hereafter are from Catholic students and teachers in Study#1 unless otherwise stated):

> If you have non-Catholics [in the school] . . . you wouldn't want to be snobby to them saying they weren't good enough to be around . . . [and] you can benefit from that because . . . it gives you the opportunity to practice your faith in accepting people.

That concern was evident amongst the Catholic student participants in Study #1 as they asked the questions "How would I feel being in a minority? How would I want to be treated?" One Catholic student recounted an experience she had in religion class when a non-Catholic student was acting out. Seeing the non-Catholic student's behavior engendered a sincere sympathy for her confusion and lack of direction. The Catholic student said,

> She was in Christian ethics class. She was bitter about it [bring in class]: not respectful towards the Catholic faith . . . she sat in the back of the class and made sarcastic comments . . . It was aimless rebellion . . . She was creating that feeling [of separateness although] there was no exclusion coming from us or any hard feelings towards her regarding faith . . . I felt really bad for her because she was obviously really confused and it seemed like she wanted answers but she was going about it in the totally wrong way.

In general, in Study #1, it appears that Catholic students empathized with the non-Catholic students' sense of being the Other and sought to alleviate it. Further, it seemed evident that Catholic students in Study #1 wanted to avoid the perception that they were the anointed ones within their school and emphasized the rights of non-Catholic students, one Catholic students saying, "Everybody has to practice their own beliefs, that's freedom of speech and [they] . . . should be allowed to come to school and express [their] . . . opinion." However, in a lighter moment in Study #1, one Catholic student remarked that once a non-Catholic student in his class was being rather difficult by challenging the Catholic faith. The Catholic student said, "I feel bad for him cause when he dies all the stuff he says will come back to kick him in the head."

In sum, the Catholic high school students recognized, respected, and at times empathized with non-Catholic students' sense of being "different" within their high schools. The Catholic student was psychologically affected by the presence of non-Catholic students within the school.

The Catholic Teacher

Catholic teachers in Study #1, from which all of the following quotations are drawn unless stated otherwise, experienced psychological effects attributable to inclusion.

Catholic teachers recognized that non-Catholic students face being a minority within the school and there was both empathy for their sense of being the "other," and for their courage should they participate in liturgical services. One teacher related,

> Sometimes I wonder how welcome non-Catholic students feel. I've never felt a sense or feeling of [their] not being welcome. That question of I'm not Catholic and therefore he [the teacher] sees me as a second-class citizen . . . I don't think they feel that way, but I can see where that might happen.

This empathy was a new phenomenon to at least one participating school administrator, who stated, "Over the last few years . . . there's more of an awareness or empathy for how the [non-Catholic] kids feel being different, and do we make them feel different or uncomfortable. But I don't think we do."

The above evidences a sense of concern engendered by the Catholic teacher's self reflection as was reiterated in some teachers' belief that there was no good reason to be told which students were non-Catholic. One teacher said, "I don't record it [if being non-Catholic is disclosed] and I don't make a point of remembering it . . . To prevent bias by me . . . [or] that they feel it." This teacher expressed the view that not knowing the religion of the students in his class removed possible teacher bias, actual or perceived, and ensured the comfort level of the non-Catholic student in that she or he would not feeling publicly "marked" as different.

Certainly inclusion engendered self reflectivity amongst some Catholic teachers. One teacher related the following story. When on a retreat with Catholic and non-Catholic students who were open and challenging in their discussions the teacher stated, "You're challenged to look at yourself and say, 'What do I really believe?'"

In summation, Catholic high school teachers in Study #1 certainly recognized the potential sense of "otherness" which could be experienced by the non-Catholic students, and empathized with that possible plight and indeed sought to protect the student or at least to alleviate that anxiety if it existed within the non-Catholic student school body. Concurrently, the psychological effects upon the Catholic teacher were to deepen her or his own faith and to see beyond denominational barriers which as a result increased acceptance of various beliefs and blurred differences amongst religious beliefs and emphasized orthopraxis over orthodoxy.

The psychological affects of inclusion on Catholic teachers in Study #1 emphasized self-reflection, empathy, a sense of protection extended to the Other and a sincere desire to exhibit acceptance into the school community.

The Non-Catholic Student

This part of Chapter Eight looks at the psychological effects of inclusion upon non-Catholic students. However, due to the low rates of participation in the studies, (Study #3, Study #4) which ground these emergent themes it seems prudent to consider the following as possible or potential indicators of the psychological effects of inclusion upon non-Catholic high school students.

There are three possible affects which emerged from the research: the engendering of a sense of reflectivity, an intense feeling of alienation from the school community, and the embedding of a subliminal lasting affect in the minds of some non-Catholic students.

Reflectivity

A non-Catholic student from Study #2 related the significance of Morning Prayer in the school,

> the more that you're exposed to that [the idea of God] the more you're reminded [of God]. Whether it's through morning prayer or Mass . . . I think that helps bring you back on to the right path, its a reminder about what's important.

Alienation from Community

A non-Catholic student from that study and from a home where religion was not important stated: "the [in-school religious] services were boring." Whereas another participant whose family eschewed religion, and had attended the Catholic high school only because it was closer to his home than a public high school stated,

> Everyone went up to get communion and there would be like ten of us sitting there and everyone would look at all of us because we didn't get up. How exclusive can you be! I mean it's horrible to like sit . . . and everyone just looks at you like you're crazy. I'm definitely angry at my four years [in Catholic high school] . . . very, very angry.

Lasting Effects

Seeley (2000) found in her study that "most of the [non-Catholic student] participants' responses to questions about Catholicism as a formal religion were either negative or neutral" (p. 85). This researcher's findings in Study #3 concur. However, it is an interesting phenomenon that two of the nine participants in that Study chose after graduation to work as teaching assistants in Catholic high schools. One of the students came from a religiously committed family and the other comes from a non-committed family. Their comments were as follows:

> . . . perhaps like a plant. It doesn't think about the fact that there's water or that there's sunlight, but it's there and it's affected by it. [It has] to have some affect because you know, just a lot of times you're learning how to relate to other people . . . how to converse and get along . . . through Catholic morals and it probably has a bit of an affect that you don't even realize.

> Nobody's forcing you to talk a certain way, think a certain way . . . but you know it's an impact whether or not you notice it or not.

Two non-Catholic students noted the lasting positive effects of attending a Catholic high school. The first said, as quoted earlier, "it helped me deepen my strength and it helped me deepen my relationship with Christ."

The second was asked by the researcher, "Did going to a Catholic high school affect your faith?" The student responded, "Yes, definitely. You're taught in a way that you develop yourself spiritually."

Interestingly, one scholar (Seeley, 2000) has suggested that "Catholic schools seem to have their effect on those who attend them not so much through formal religious instruction class but rather through the closeness of the Catholic community that the experiences of attending Catholic school generates" (p. 167). That comment seems to be intuitively correct from the experiences of this researcher in Study #3 and Study #4.

Although the following is tentative, it seems that it is possible that if the non-Catholic student's family was at all committed to their own religious faith there was a possibility that after four years of exposure and immersion in religious symbolism, rituals, and language there could be a positive spiritual effect, perhaps subliminal in nature, upon that student evident within a few years of graduation. This is a very important and very tentative finding which deserves more research on a much wider scale than this study has provided. Perhaps it quietly speaks to the new evangelization in the Catholic Church (Boyack, 1992) in terms of the non-Catholic student.

There is much more work to be done with respect to the psychological dimension of inclusion. In particular, it is significant that the research has demonstrated that it is the peer group which is of the greatest significance to the non-Catholic students – at least those in high school.

PART II

Part II offers a few brief thoughts on the significance of those findings in Part I with the works of Harris (1998), Erickson (1950), Kohlberg (1981), and Gilligan (1982).

Harris

This book has stated the importance of a Catholic school's faith community to the experience of Catholic education for students. Indeed, the faith community may be seen as the *sine qua non* of the Catholic school. Yet, there is evidence that the most important community to the student, Catholic and non-Catholic, within the Catholic school is the peer community. Traditionally the belief has been that the triangle of family, church, and school was the foundation upon which the Catholic child would be acculturated or socialized into the Catholic faith. That assumption may now be challenged by recent writings from one author – Judith Harris (1998). Her position is that it is the peer group within which the child finds herself or himself that determines the personality of the child. Harris states in her book *The Nurture Assumption: Why Children Turn Out the Way That They Do*, "I believe the human mind has at least two different departments for dealing with social behaviour. One has to do with personal relationships; the other has to do with groups (p. 361)".

> In the peer groups of childhood and adolescence, kids take on the behaviours and attitudes of their peers and contrast themselves with the members of other groups – groups that differ in sex or race or social class or in their propensities and interests . . . Children learn about themselves by comparing themselves to their group mates . . . They are typecast by their peers. . . Experiences in childhood and adolescent peer groups modify children's personalities in ways they will carry with them to adulthood . . . Group socialization theory makes this prediction: that children would develop into the same adults if we left their lives outside the home unchanged – left them in their schools and their neighborhoods – but switched all the parents around. (p. 359)

If Harris is correct then the theory behind the enculturation of Catholic students into the Catholic faith via the school as a Catholic institution and the acceptance and integration, but not assimilation nor evangelization, of the non-Catholic student into the Catholic school community may be due a second look. Indeed, based upon her theory, to achieve its objectives, the Catholic school should retain the visual, auditory, and experiential aspects of the evangelization of Catholic students and the overt welcoming of non-Catholic students once they have been admitted to the school but, thereafter, the focus should be upon influencing the nature of the small peer groups of students within the school in a manner consistent with the behaviors expected of the Catholic faith. That is a huge and perhaps next to impossible task but if Harris is correct, it is the most effective, if not the only effective, means of influencing the socialization of both Catholic and non-Catholic students within the Catholic school. The quotations presented earlier in this Chapter indicate that it is the students' sense of belonging and needing to belong and relating to those with whom they feel connected – their peers – is of the greatest importance to them.

Erikson

Erikson's (1950) concept of the adolescent crisis of identity and role confusion from approximately 11 to 18 years of age argues for the Catholic school to attend carefully not just to the pedagogical and cognitive aspects of the student but also the emotional domain. Within that area, it is suggested, that the self identity of the student is being forged within the crucible of adolescent social life within the individual's peer group. That is the time the student will ask "Who am I? Where do I fit in with those important to me? Where am I going in my life?" The sense of confusion and exploration, anxiety, angst, and excitement make adolescence a time of change – of metamorphosis not only physically, cognitively, emotionally, and socially, but also spiritually.

Catholic students who encounter others who are of differing religious faiths experience a variety of emotions and cognitive conundrums which vary from student to student. However, it is also important to understand that the Catholic students, although usually in the majority within the Catholic school, do not, as evidenced by my research findings, want to be perceived as oppressive or as a cult to themselves by non-Catholics within the school and without. Catholic students are very willing to enter into the conversation about faith and religion and God with non-Catholic students as long as there is mutual respect amongst those in conversation. However, the evidence is that such conversations are not the *sine qua non* of relationships amongst students within Catholic schools whether Catholic students, non-Catholic students, or a combination thereof.

Table 3. Erickson's Stages of Human Development

Chart adapted from Erikson's 1959 *Identity and the Life Cycle* (Psychological Issues vol 1, #1)
Retrieved May 14, 2008 from http://webspace.ship.edu/cgboer/erikson.html
Dr. C. George Boeree Ph.D. Oklahoma State University
Shippensburg University
1871 Old Main Drive
Shippensburg, PA 17257
(717)-477-7447

Stage (age)	Psychosocial crisis	Significant relations	Psychosocial modalities	Psychosocial virtues	Maladaptations & malignancies
I (0 to 1) infant	trust vs mistrust	Mother	to get, to give in return	hope, faith	sensory distortion – withdrawal
II (2 to 3) toddler	autonomy vs shame and doubt	Parents	to hold on, to let go	will, determination	impulsivity – compulsion
III (3 to 6) preschooler	initiative vs guilt	Family	to go after, to play	purpose, courage	ruthlessness – inhibition
IV (7 to 12 or so) school-age child	industry vs inferiority	neighborhood and school	to complete, to make things together	competence	narrow virtuosity – inertia
V (12 to 18 or so) adolescence	ego-identity vs role-confusion	peer groups, role models	to be oneself, to share oneself	fidelity, loyalty	fanaticism – repudiation
VI (the 20s) young adult	intimacy vs isolation	partners, friends	to lose and find oneself in a another	love	promiscuity – exclusivity
VII (late 20s to 50s) middle adult	generativity vs self-absorption	Household, workmates	to make be, to take care of	care	overextension – rejectivity
VIII (50s and beyond) old adult	integrity vs despair	mankind or "my kind"	to be, through having been, to face not being	wisdom	presumption – despair

Kohlberg

Erickson's staged development seems to fit, at least in part, with Kohlberg's (1981) stages of moral development. In particular, the Catholic students' reaction to the presence of non-Catholic students within their schools indicate that the conventional stage and post conventional stages were reached by the Catholic student participants in Study #1. In concert with the Conventional Stage there was certainly the sense from Catholic students that there was a desire to maintain good relationships and to help others and to maintain the existing social order of acceptance within the Catholic school as espoused by the school authorities. However, the evidence also exhibited some Catholic students as having reached the post conventional stage beyond the social contract or legalistic areas to the level of conscience and universal principles. In particular, ideas such as justice, equality, and a respect for the dignity of each individual within the school, Catholic and non-Catholic, were evident in the responses of some Catholic students.

This was also the case with some of the non-Catholic students who saw beyond their own religious belief system and accepted the value of the Catholic students' beliefs not as valid or true but as non-threatening to their own beliefs.

Kohlberg suggested that a stimulus was required to cause one to move beyond a particular stage of moral development and it is clear in my research that the inclusion on non-Catholic students into Catholic schools provides such a catalyst.

Table 4. Kohlberg's Stages of Moral Development

Approximate Age Range	**Stage**	**Substages**
Birth to 9	Pre-conventional	1) Avoid punishment 2) Gain Reward
Age 9 to 20	Conventional	3) Gain Approval & Avoid Disapproval 4) Duty & Guilt
Age 20+ maybe never	Post-conventional	5) Agreed upon rights 6) Personal moral standards

Note: Retrieved May 25, 2008 from www.stolaf.edu/people/huff/classes/handbook/Gilligan.html

Gilligan

It would be remiss not to state that Kohlberg has had his critics, one of whom was a close associate. Gilligan (1982) has argued, amongst other things, that Kohlberg's stages of moral development were male and justice based and that the stages of moral reasoning for women was different. She stated,

> The elusive mystery of women's development lies in its recognition of the continuing importance of attachment in the human life-cycle. Woman's place in man's life cycle is to protect this recognition while the [masculine] development litany intones the celebration of separation, autonomy,

> individualism, and natural rights . . . Only when life-cycle theories divide their attention and begin to live with women as they have lived with men will their vision encompass the experience of both sexes and their theories become correspondingly more fertile. (p. 23)

Gilligan's point is well made – especially as Kohlberg's seminal work involved only male participants. Practically, Gilligan's Stages of moral reasoning found that their moral reasoning was focused upon a concern for relationships, attachments, and self-sacrifice and suggested a different set of stages than did Kohlberg. Both are presented at the end of this Chapter. Suffice to say that in attempting to understand the psychological nuances of the inclusion of non-Catholic students into Catholic schools it seems necessary to understand the psychological effects on the Catholic students, teachers, and the non-Catholic students. Overarching all is the responsibility and the ethic of care (Noddings, 1984) owed by those within the institution of Catholic education to all whose lives are so intensely and intimately effected by it.

Table 5. Gilligan's Stages of Moral Development

Approximate Age Range	Stage	Goal
Not listed	Pre-conventional	Goal is individual survival
Transition is from selfishness – to – responsibility to others		
Not listed	Conventional	Self sacrifice is goodness
Transition is from goodness – to – truth that she is a person too		
maybe never	Post-conventional	Principle of nonviolence: do not hurt others or self

Note: Retrieved May 25, 2008 from www.stolaf.edu/people/huff/classes/handbook/Gilligan.html

PART III

The development of faith whether viewed in stages (Fowler, 1981) or through an existential revelation leading to conviction (Loder, 1998) is relevant to the topic of inclusion as that phenomenon affects the psychology of non-Catholic and Catholic students as well as Catholic teachers and others. Further the evangelization of Catholic students is arguably intrinsically involved with an understanding of the psychology of adolescence and human growth. The protection, teaching, and nurturing of non-Catholic students is also of primary importance and as faith and religion surround the non-Catholic student in the Catholic school it seems incumbent to attempt to understand the relationship of faith and the development of children whether they be Catholic or non-Catholic.

The following sections briefly state Fowler's Stages of Faith and Loder's Transforming Moment of Faith.

Fowler's Stages of Faith

Fowler (1981) states,

> I believe that faith is a human universal. We are endowed at birth with nascent capacities for faith. How these capacities are activated and grow depends to a large extent on how we are welcomed into the world and what kinds of environments we grow in. Faith is interactive and social; it requires community, language, ritual and nurture. Faith is also shaped by initiatives from beyond us and other people, initiatives of spirit or grace. How these latter initiatives are recognized and imaged, or unperceived and ignored, powerfully affects the shape of faith in our lives. (p. xiii)

Fowler was greatly influenced by Kohlberg and viewed the human as being capable of moving through a series of stages in her or his life from the "primal faith" of infancy to the "universalized faith" which was possible from "mid-life and beyond" (Fowler, 1991, pp. 24 – 25). As in Kohlberg's theory, an individual does not necessarily move in sequence through stages as one could become stuck at a stage. The stages offered by Fowler are represented in the following chart.

Fowler's Stages of Faith

A Brief Summary	Explanation
Primal Faith (Infancy)	"A prelanguage disposition of trust forms in the mutuality of one's relationships with parents and others to offset the anxiety that results from separations which occur during infant development" (Fowler, 1991, p. 24).
Stage 1 **Intuitive-Projective Faith** **(Early Childhood)**	"Imagination, stimulated by stories, gestures, and symbols, and not yet controlled by logical thinking, combines with perception and feelings to create long-lasting images that represent both the protective and threatening powers surrounding one's life" (Fowler, 1991, p. 24).
Stage 2 **Mythic-Literal Faith** **(Childhood and Beyond)**	"The developing ability to think logically helps one order the world with categories of causality, space, and time; to enter into the perspectives of others; and to capture life meaning in stories" (Fowler, 1991, pp. 24, 25).
Stage 3 **Synthetic-Conventional Faith** **(Adolescence and Beyond)**	"New cognitive abilities make mutual perspective taking possible and require one to integrate diverse self-images into a coherent identity. A personal and largely unreflective synthesis of beliefs and values evolves to support identity and to unite one in emotional solidarity with others" (Fowler, 1991, p. 25).
Stage 4 **Individuative-Reflective Faith** **(Young Adulthood and Beyond)**	"Critical reflection upon one's beliefs and values, utilizing third-person perspective taking; understanding of the self and others as part of a social system; the internalization of authority and the assumption of responsibility for making explicit choices of ideology and life-style; all open the way for critically self-aware commitments in relationships and vocation" (Fowler, 1991, p. 25).

Fowler's Stages of Faith (continued)

Stage 5 **Conjunctive Faith** **(Mid-life and Beyond)**	"The embrace of polarities in one's life, alertness to paradox, and the need for multiple interpretations of reality mark this stage. Symbol and story, metaphor and myth (from one's own traditions and others') are newly appreciated (second or willed naïveté) as vehicles for expressing truth" (Fowler, 1991, p. 25).
Stage 6 **Universalizing Faith** **(Mid-life and Beyond)**	"Beyond paradox and polarities, persons in this stage are grounded in a oneness with the power of being. Their visions and commitments free them for a passionate yet detached spending of the self in love, devoted to overcoming division, oppression, and violence, and in effective anticipatory response to an inbreaking commonwealth of love and justice" (Fowler, 1991, p. 25).

For the purposes of this book, the most relevant stage is Stage 3 and in some cases Stage 4. As Fowler (1981) says "Stage 3 typically has its rise and ascendancy in adolescence, but for many adults it becomes a permanent place of equilibrium" (pp. 172, 173). At this stage, the individual has not formulated an ideology or cosmology but it is nevertheless sensed and experienced by the individual. This "Synthetic-Conventional Faith" is conformist is nature and not yet critically examined but rather is merely experienced. However, in the next stage, the "Individuative-Reflective Faith" the adolescent or young adult faces the paradoxes and challenges of living in a complex social world where,

> the person must face certain unavoidable tensions: individuality versus being defined by a group or group membership; subjectivity and the power of one's strongly felt but unexamined feelings versus objectivity and the requirement of critical reflection; self-fulfillment or self-actualization as a primary concern versus service to and being for others; the question of being committed to the relative versus struggle with the possibility of the absolute. (Fowler, 1981, p. 182)

It was my experience, through my research in Western Canadian Catholic high schools, that Catholic students in Grade 10 were at a Stage 3 level but somewhere during Grades 11 and 12 many Catholic students were in part pushed into Stage 4 due to the presence of non-Catholic students in the Catholic high school. Stage 3 is the conformist stage where the student's cosmology is defined primarily by authorities as the self is in the process of formation. The presence of non-Catholic students in Catholic high schools may be a catalyst for intellectual and spiritual and faith growth into Stage 4. It is in Stage 4 that the adolescent or young adult takes personal responsibility for her or his beliefs, values, and life decisions (Fowler, 1981, p. 182). Hence, it is arguably difficult to live in the religious myth stage comfortably with only one story when confronted with equally powerful stories from one's peers. This is the stage of the awakening of the individual's sense of critical reflection which, when encountering the Other, surely would engender asking the questions "Why do I believe what I believe?"

It would be misleading to only offer the reader Fowler's approach to the development of faith as so Loder's (1998) position follows hereafter.

Loder's Transforming Moment of Faith

Loder (1998) takes issue with Fowler's staged development of faith, saying,

> It is generally assumed that the transformational process is in the service of and dependent on the stages of development. This is surely true where ego development and inherited structural potentials are concerned, but it is not fundamentally true. The transformational process is more fundamental in that it may (1) transcend the stages, reversing arrested development and reinstating repressed structures; also (2) it may leap ahead by passing stages and establish an imaginative basis for development that incorporates but is not restricted to the so-called normal sequence. In effect, I am suggesting a figure-ground reversal with respect to stages and proves. Whereas most studies of development are concerned to map the stages and leave process to itself, this discussion is concerned primarily with the integrity of the process. . . . we actually spend most of our lives in transition than we do in equilibrium. . . . ." (p. 130)

For Loder, the mechanical approach of the developmentalists fails to consider that human beings spend most of their time between the offered stages. Moreover, if one assumes a divine creator with a personal interest in the individual as well as free will, it is the moment of conviction which may be triggered by the divine or by a radical act of free will which can produce a profound understanding through experience of one faith – which is, I submit, a relationship with the divine. This is what I suggest Loder means when he says that the person undergoing such a "convictional" experience "is breaking into a new order of reality" (Loder, 1998, pp. 16, 17) [emphasis added]. In an existential moment Loder (1998) states that such experiences are,

> beyond naturalistic study and should be recognized and accepted as such, except where personality disintegration is being imposed by the experience. . . . this claim and the exception raise many questions about normality, disintegration, and the ecstatic. . . . I only want to point out the irony implicit in the human sciences' effort to investigate a phenomenon that in its own right challenges the major assumptions on which the human sciences work. (pp.16–17)

There is truth in what Loder says. The quotations stated earlier in this Chapter illustrate that such moments of conviction occur in Catholic schools both for Catholic students and teachers as well as non-Catholic students. Certainly a deepening of conviction of Catholic students and teachers and non-Catholic students was evident at least for some participants of the studies referred to in this book. If faith development is associated with human development, as suggested by Fowler and not denied but supplemented in understanding the phenomenon of the actualization of faith by Loder, then the psychological effects of the convictional moment may well be triggered – at least at times – by inclusion – for Catholic students, teachers and non-Catholic students in the Catholic high school.

SUMMARY

Arguably, the psychological effects of inclusion on those within the Catholic school vary according to the individual's psychological stage and Stage of Faith. It is certainly true that an existential moment can thrust a student or teacher into a particular stage. It also appears to be the case that in encountering the Other reflexivity is engendered which can lead to a teacher and student entering into a critical analysis of personally held beliefs and values. In other words, inclusion appears to foster the psychological and faith development of those within the Catholic school.

CHAPTER NINE

THE NINTH DIMENSION OF INCLUSION: SPIRITUAL

Chapter Nine deals with the spiritual dimension and begins with various understandings of the term spirituality within the Catholic faith. It then moves on to provide quotations from Catholic students and teachers which manifest their expression of spirituality within their schools in relation to the inclusion of non-Catholic students.

THE TERM: SPIRITUALITY

Maher and Bolland, (1912) suggest that the term spirituality in Catholicism relates to the soul as separate and apart from the body. They say,

> The question of the reality of the soul and its distinction from the body is among the most important problems of philosophy, for with it is bound up the doctrine of a future life. Various theories as to the nature of the soul have claimed to be reconcilable with the tenet of immortality, but it is a sure instinct that leads us to suspect every attack on the substantiality or spirituality of the soul as an assault on the belief in existence after death. The soul may be defined as the ultimate internal principle by which we think, feel, and will, and by which our bodies are animated. The term "mind" usually denotes this principle as the subject of our conscious states, while "soul" denotes the source of our vegetative activities as well. That our *vital activities proceed from a principle capable of subsisting in itself is the thesis of the substantiality of the soul: that this principle is not itself composite, extended, corporeal, or essentially and intrinsically dependent on the body, is the doctrine of spirituality* [emphasis added].

Catholic spirituality, therefore, relates to the soul but it has also been seen as involving various practices such as in the *Spiritual Exercises of St. Ignatius* (Debuchy, 1912),

> The [above] book is composed of documents or spiritual exercises, reduced to the order most fitted to move the minds of the faithful to piety, as was remarked in the Brief of approval. We find in this work documents (instruct-tions, admonitions, warnings), exercises (prayers, meditations examination of conscience, and other practices), and the method according to which they are arranged. The sources of the book are the Sacred Scriptures and the experiences of spiritual life.

In Catholic pedagogy, the spiritual dimension has recently been noted by Nuzzi (2004b) where he pointed to the connection between spirituality, religious instruction, and provides a review of the leading theorists in that area. My research (Studies #1, #2, #3, #4) reaffirmed the importance of the spiritual element to Catholic education but also determined that the phenomenon of inclusion impacts that spiritual dimension and should therefore be considered by Catholic schools.

Secular and Sacred Spirituality

Noddings (1998-1999) speaks of the difference between spirituality and religion, at least in so far as the secular school system is concerned, saying, "Spirituality is an attitude or a way of life that recognizes something we might call spirit. Religion is a specific way of exercising that spirituality and usually requires an institutional affiliation. Spirituality does not require an institutional connection" (p. 1).

Groome (1998) suggests that,

> In Christian tradition, the spirit in spirituality is also God's Spirit. The Holy Spirit moves within human spirits to entice us into relationship with God and to allow this primary relationship to permeate all relationships – with self, others, and the world. Christian spirituality, then, is a partnership between God's Spirit and human spirits – working in kinship. Spiritual growth is a lifelong journey, sustained by God's Spirit through our own, into living as a people of God. (p. 325)

The difference between the two definitions is striking. Nodding's spirituality is singular, individualized, whereas Groome's definition requires as a prerequisite, *community* and r*elationship* with others, especially the Holy Spirit. This is consistent with what Groome calls a Christian cosmology (Groome, 1998, pp. 118-126). It was Groome's perspective which was evident in both the teacher and student focus groups in Study #1.

One might say that Catholic spirituality assumes the existence of the soul created by God (Maher and Bollaand, 1912), which is in relationship with the Holy Spirit (Groome, 1998), in community interacting with others (Debuchy, 1912), experiencing the Spirit's Gifts (wisdom, understanding, knowledge, counsel, fortitude, piety, fear of the Lord – corresponding to the capital virtues of charity, faith, prudence, fortitude, justice, and hope (Aquinas, 1948, II.2). That understanding of spirituality is indeed very different from secular concepts or cultist formulations of the concept. It is the acknowledgement of the spiritual nature of being human (the individual soul) in relationship with God as expressed in the Spirit.

Expressing Spirituality in Schools

The term spirituality is used in this dimension as faith experienced by the participants.

One Christian ethics teacher remarked, in recounting a story involving a contentious non-Catholic student in a Christian ethics class:

> [non-Catholic] kids, . . . their faith has been made stronger by having that individual in my class, and my faith and my knowledge has increased tenfold since the beginning of this semester, because I'm on my toes, more aware, and having to explain the Catholic faith more because he's in my class . . . He challenges everyone in the class, for good though. At the beginning of the class, it was annoying. I'll say it was annoying! He stimulates conversation, and if anything, I'm more excited to go to my church on Sunday (Study #1).

Teachers (Donlevy, 2007b) have had moving spiritual experiences in their relationships with non-Catholic students which constitute the assimilation of them into the school community and a merger of faiths, as opposed to religions, such that, as an issue, inclusively appears to disappear and certainly becomes moot for many Catholic teachers "When you have a non-Catholic kid, who you know is non-Catholic, come to you and ask you to pray for her family, you know you've done something beyond just Catholicism. There's more to it than just being Catholic" (Study #1).

The idea of a symbiotic spiritual relationship between Catholic and non-Catholic students was stated by a Grade 12 Catholic student.

> You feed off each other, and if all your feeding [is from the] people . . . who are the same as you, that is good, but it can only offer you so much. But when you have people with different views – different beliefs, it heightens yours and it brings them up at the same time so everyone just grows . . . maybe not in the same direction of growth but you will grow to a better understanding and more mature life (Study #1).

Included in the above comment was the concept of opportunity, both for the non-Catholic student to grow in an understanding of the Catholic faith, and for the Catholic student to practice her or his faith. A Grade 12 Catholic student related, "It's good to have someone to challenge our faith and to have someone to help make us stronger" (Study #1).

Moreover, it was the presence of the non-Catholic student, and the relationships which Catholic students had with their non-Catholic friends in the school, which demanded that the Catholic student listen and accept the "others" as persons and thus live the ideals or beliefs of acceptance, understanding, and respect. To quote one Grade 11 Catholic student, "We need these people [the non-Catholics] to put into practice Jesus' teachings" (Study #1).

It was clear that, in the case of the majority of the student participants in Study #1, spirituality meant faith and faith meant experiences which were related to something communal, larger than the individual, based upon relationships and to which they were emotionally affected. Religion was a conceptual construction proffered to them by teachers and the Catholic Church. The Catholic teachers in Study #1 were more closely divided and tended to perceive spirituality or faith as the lived experience of a religion; not necessarily the Catholic religion. As earlier stated, Groome's (1998) perspective was present in both the teacher and student focus group sessions. It is this "phenomenological approach" to a spirituality of faith, orthopraxis, rather than what many saw as the pre-Vatican II catechetical approach, orthodoxy or catechesis, that dominated the focus group sessions (Rummery, 2001).

Study #1 confirmed Nuzzi's (2004b) statement that, "the spiritual quest of many young adults can properly be understood as a search for more instruction and more catechesis, for more information and more personal relevance" (p. 68). This topic is discussed in more detail under the tenth (philosophical) dimension.

IN SUMMARY

There is much more to be said about spirituality as a dimension of inclusion. Surely it should be – in the future – considered in conjunction with the Stages of Faith as delineated by Fowler (1981, 1991) and the force of argument and revelation of the impact of faith as described by Loden (1998). However, for the purposes of this book, the term spirituality may be seen as a fundamental characteristic of the human soul which exists within and yet is part of the entity which is also physical. It may be reached through the physical, emotional, and intellectual domains, but to be fully realized, it must be in communion with the Holy Spirit. Further research is warranted in the area of spirituality, children, and Catholic schools and there is evidence that the topic of children and spirituality with reference to Catholic schools has begun (Erricker, J, et al, 2001; see also the *International Journal of Children's Spirituality*). Certainly the issue of spirituality in the Catholic faith is complex and of long standing (Aumann, 1985) and Christian spirituality in general has been re-visited by some authors (Cunningham and Egan, 1996).

CHAPTER TEN

THE TENTH DIMENSION OF INCLUSION: PHILOSOPHICAL

The Tenth Dimension of inclusion deals with the question "How does inclusion affect the philosophical understandings of the faith of Catholic students, Catholic teachers, and non-Catholic students?" In answering that question, this Chapter utilizes the data from Studies #1, #3, and #4 as well as referencing various scholarly articles and books.

CATHOLIC STUDENTS: THEIR FAITH AND INCLUSION

In Study #1 there was clear evidence that some Catholic students believed that inclusion was a lived concept of greater importance then a sense of individual faith as expressed in a particular religion such as Catholicism. One Catholic student responded to the question "Who did Jesus come to save?" as follows.

> I just want to say that Jesus didn't come for the Christians. There weren't any. He came for the Gentiles . . . He came for the poor people of the time, the people who did not believe in God . . . He spent His life for those people. He lived for those people and not to convert them to Christianity. He wanted to convert them to love . . . I think that's this school . . . And other people who sort of embody the spirit of Jesus like Mahatma Ghandi, [who] all his life he spent trying, promoting unity between the faiths and he spent his time not with the other Hindus or Muslims trying to get along, but he spent time with the untouchables. [If Christ comes again, is He coming back as a Catholic?] I'm sure He's not. I'm sure He's not (Study #1).

However, not all Catholic students were so liberal in the approach to believing conversion to brotherly and sisterly love was equivalent to conversion to Catholicism. For some Catholic students such a liberal approach to the Gospel could foster syncretism and was, therefore, not appropriate in a Catholic school. The students' debate was as follows.

> I think [listening to and debating non-Catholic's religious beliefs is] keeping an open mind. God is a very personal thing, even to different Catholics. God has many different faces. That's why the Hindu faith has so many different gods; they're all expressions of the one God which is so difficult to understand. Part of the problem in teaching our faith is that God is a very personal thing and people come to know God in very different ways. I don't think you can say an expression of God is wrong when you are teaching. You

> cannot say to your students that, "your idea is not really correct and that this is the correct idea of God" (Study #1).

In response, another student said,

> I agree that open-mindedness is important in a Christian ethics classroom, but I also think that there is a really fine line between great discussions and open discussions where almost every Catholic belief is . . . thrown out the window just for the sake of a good discussion . . . My experience with some of my teachers [has been], even though the discussions might be really intriguing, is that Catholic values are not enforced [in class discussion]. Everyone interprets God differently. [But] I still don't know if being that open minded is really beneficial to the God of Catholic education . . . The Catholic school is not meant to be a moral or spiritual neutral zone (Study #1).

In sum, Catholic students' sense of their faith as expressed through the Catholic religion was at times tested by the presence of non-Catholic students in the Catholic school. Such testing was, as described earlier, generally positive but not if the foundations of Catholicism were allowed to suffer from syncretism.

CATHOLIC TEACHERS: THEIR FAITH AND INCLUSION

Catholic teachers were not immune from having their sense of faith and the beliefs which underpinned that faith affected by inclusion. One teacher stated,

> I was thinking back to our Catholic Education picture [which the researcher had each participant draw] and I was thinking how that picture would be different from . . . A Christian Education picture. And, I'm struggling here, as I'm trying to differentiate between the two. Oh, I know Catholics are Christians, but as a particular faith, how would that picture differ? And maybe that's why we don't get a lot of opposition [in society for Catholic education] . . . I think we are more Christian than Catholic (Study #1).

Another teacher was quick to respond:

> Oh, I don't know about that. I think we're probably, based on my experience in teaching, and the way we were raised, I think our Catholic schools are not conservative Catholic institutions, or that we are conservative. We're middle-of-the-road. We're not ultra-conservative institutions and we're not at the very liberal end. We're pretty much middle-of-the-road, and I'd say that the presentation of Catholicism in our schools is moderate, middle-of-the-road. And therefore when I present a picture of Catholic education or a Catholic school, that would have less traditional symbols in it, be more post-Vatican II. That's what I see as a picture of our identity, not pre-Vatican II [images] (Study #1).

The differentiation of the Catholic faith from other Christian faiths certainly perplexed teachers. One view was that it was the Church's tradition and activity in social action that distinguished the Catholic faith from its Christian counterparts.

> I go back to the tradition, which is where the Church is rooted . . . it goes back to the early Church and that is the basis on which we stand . . . I think it's basically who we are . . . We're coming with all of our flaws in the Church . . . And all of our successes and our leadership . . . In health care, and education and lots of development of European civilization . . . So I think we have a strong basis of social action and a sense of doing things within the world. We are called out to bring Jesus to others and not stand around waiting for others to come to us (Study #1).

A statement from a Christian ethics teacher perhaps best captures how most teachers from all the sessions felt about this dimension.

> I don't think at this level of education we offer a theological basis beyond kids understanding, and I think we provide, in the Catholic school system, a very strong foundation of faith and Jesus and God and the teachings of Christ. I don't think we go beyond that to a theological stretch [saying] that we can't include all religions in what we see in these children, these students, non-Catholic, Catholic whatever they are. [We are] providing a very sound foundation in the teachings of Christ and a foundation they can apply to any faith that comes into our building (Study #1).

Related to the Catholic-Christian dichotomy, one teacher said,

> Years ago, there was a sense of what a Protestant meant as opposed to Catholic. And I think we all knew what that meant. But the society we live in now is secular, and a lot of those definitions, when I was growing-up . . . there really isn't that sense anymore, and that's probably a good thing, because so many things that I think people saw as divisions or see as divisions, [are not and] we are now looking at what brings us together, not what's different (Study #1).

In response to the question, "Are there differences?" one teacher responded with what was on some teachers' minds, who questioned the above position,

> Well, if there aren't [any differences] then it shouldn't be relevant whether or not I'm Catholic, as long as I'm Christian. What makes me unique as a Catholic? . . . I went to a . . . religious school, a multi-denominational school where virtually everybody belonged to a church. The expectation was different, should be different [in the Catholic school]. If it isn't, why bother to define what Catholic is and what isn't Catholic (Study #1)?

This theme remained a murky and contentious area throughout the teacher sessions in Study #1. The traditional position was that the purpose of Catholic education was to instill the Catholic faith in students, in other words, to evangelize youth into the Faith. As one teacher stated,

> I guess I feel that my purpose is to evangelize. That's part of what I'm directed to do by the Church, to teach in a Catholic school, and regardless of their background, Catholic or non-Catholic, that is my purpose, to evangelize (Study #1).

Another commented, "Our mandate is to teach Catholicism and not just Christianity." Indeed, the mandate for the Catholic school was seen by that teacher as given by the Catholic Church,

> My understanding of our history is that our mandate as a school system is an extension of the family of the faith . . . that's clearly the mandate of the Church. It wasn't just to say God loves everybody and we all go to heaven (Study #1).

The second position was quite different. In response to the question, "From whom does the mandate come?" one teacher responded:

> From the parents. The Catholic community wants this institution to exist. They've wanted it to exist, and I'm not sure if there's been a reality check lately. You look at the negative reaction to the Catholic schools . . . but you sometimes wonder whether people really are giving it a lot of thought. As educators we are aware of what our mandate is, because we are Catholic. I think it's social justice. The things that we show kids helps define us as more than just Christian. It's social justice. Not that there's no social justice in public schools, but I think that's something our Christian ethics department works very hard at . . . social justice (Study #1).

The third position is quite different from the first two and is humanist in approach. Several teachers saw the purpose of Catholic education as instilling basic human values, primarily the golden rule, into their students. One Christian ethics teacher said:

> I don't care what faith anyone is . . . I tell my kids this, as long as we're all working towards making this world a better place, to the best of our ability, that's all that God, your God, my God, can ask. I hope that's what my faith reflects to the students I teach . . . I think that respect is the key. That's what I want my kids to know, that regardless of what you believe, as long as you are living life to the best of your ability and you're living a positive life, then you're living a life of faith and that's all I ask . . . I'm looking to the day where I get in trouble for that because that's what I teach in my Christian ethics class. I don't believe you have to be a Catholic to get to heaven. As long as I'm willing to walk into heaven and have God introduce Himself to me as Buddha, Mohammed, whatever, I'm ready for it, as long as we're all working toward the same thing (Study #1).

Lastly, perhaps in defense of the variety of positions taken by different teachers, and a sense of frustration, a participant stated, "Catholic education does not just fall on our shoulders alone. There's the Church and the home" (Study #1).

In sum, it is fair to say that Catholic teachers have a variety of understandings of the word faith. Its meaning within the Catholic context is determined by the particular philosophical position of the teacher: fundamentalist-conservative, postmodernist, liberal. Those variations produce a multiplicity of understandings which impact upon both the mandate and the purpose of Catholic education. This divide appears evident as there is a distinction between Groome's (1998, p. 393) expression, borrowed from Joyce (1998), "Here comes everybody" to the words of *Dominus iesus*. (Congregation, 2000a, 2000b) and the voice of McLaughlin (1996) stating that with respect to Catholic education,

> [the] Catholic faith must be presented in its entirety under the guidance of the Magisterium . . . respecting the hierarchy of truths . . . and ensuring integrity of content . . . There is therefore a persistent need to discern the essential features of the Christian message which is to be transmitted to pupils . . . . (p. 143)

Perhaps Chadwick's (1994) comment has a ring of truth for some in Catholic education,

> good Roman Catholic theology no longer makes . . . absolute assertions of the exclusive claims of the Roman Catholic Church to be the only ark of salvation; there is a more positive appreciation of authentic faith and love in other Christian bodies . . . The modern concept of Church as making an appeal to the conscience, and as being more witnessing than magisterial, is certainly one that can easily be discerned in Roman Catholic writers of recent decades . . . . (p. 42)

The confusion and anxiety amongst Catholic teachers may in part be due to the paradigm shift in the role of the Catholic school teacher (Shimabukuro, 2004, pp. 126–128). It is certainly true that the difficulty in merging orthodoxy and orthopraxis is not new to Catholic education (Donlevy, 2008), Cardinal Ratzinger, as he then was, has raised the issue on three occasions. Cardinal Ratzinger (Ratzinger & Messori, 1985) stated,

> Many catechists no longer teach the Catholic faith in its harmonic wholeness . . . rather they try to make some elements of the Christian patrimony humanly 'interesting' (according to the cultural orientations of the moment). Hence it is no longer a catechesis that would constitute a comprehensive, all embracing formation in the faith, but reflections and flashes of insights deriving from the partial, subjective anthropological experiences . . . The result . . . has been a disintegration of the *sensus fidei* in the new generations, who are often incapable of a comprehensive view of their religion. (pp. 72–73)

Eleven years later Ratzinger (1996a, 1996b) twice reiterated his concern,

> There has been a collapse even of simple religious information . . . What is our catechesis doing? What is our school system doing at a time when religious instruction is widespread? I think it was an error not to pass on more

> content. Our religion instructors rightly repudiated the idea that religious instruction is only information, and they rightly said that it is something else that is more, that the point is to learn life itself that more has to be conveyed. But that led to the attempt to make people like this style of life, while information and content were neglected. Here, I think, we ought really to be ready for a change, to say that if in this secular world we have religious instruction in all the schools, we have to assume that we will not be able to convert many in schools to the faith. But the students should find out what Christianity is: they should receive good information in a sympathetic way so that they are stimulated to ask: Is this perhaps something for me? (1996a, p. 126)

Simply put, inclusion raises the issues which may already be present in some Catholic schools, the issue of "From whom does the mandate for Catholic education come?" the parents, the trustees, and/or the Church? And what is that mandate in relation to inclusion? Beyond those questions it is reasonable to ask, "Is there a threshold of inclusion beyond which the ethos of the Catholic school, the faith witness of Catholic teachers, and the evangelization of Catholic students are impaired?" and "Is there a causal relationship between the phenomenon of inclusion, at some level, and religious relativism?" This Chapter raises, but is unable to answer, those questions.

The discussions with both the student and teacher participants indicated that the philosophical differences are dealt with at the school level by what Rawls (1987) calls the "method of avoidance." He says, "we try, so far as we can, neither to assert nor to deny any religious, philosophical or moral views, or their associated philosophical accounts of truth and the status of values (pp. 12–13). As Hollenback (1996) says, this method is employed "to neutralize potential conflicts and to promote democratic social harmony" (p. 93).

NON-CATHOLIC STUDENTS: THEIR FAITH, AND INCLUSION

The impact of inclusion upon the religious beliefs of the non-Catholic students, at least in some instances, was apparent in Studies #3 and #4 as evidenced by the following quotations.

One student said,

> My religion is important to me and my family. We go to church on Sundays as a family and I attend the youth group where we pray and socialize with one another. It's good to be able to talk about Jesus and religion in school because we spend so much time there and it's not politically correct or cool [to talk about God] in public schools (Study #3).

Another related,

> You know, even though I disagreed with a lot of things said in Christian Ethics class, I think just being there and hearing the Catholic point of view makes me stronger in my own religion (Study #3).

A participant from, Study #3 stated the following with regard to prayer, liturgies, and Mass in the school:

> there was a Christian influence there and its something important to me . . . you can talk about [God] without being afraid [of] political incorrectness. . . [of being] offensive to someone else . . . That's an issue nowadays . . . what if there is someone in the room who isn't a Catholic or Christian?

A student in Study #4 stated that having prayer, liturgies, and Mass in the school, "puts or tries to put the emphasis on something else . . . something else to think about besides the normal stuff, bigger and more important than just . . . grades.

From Study #4 one student said, "Nobody's forcing you to talk a certain way, think a certain way . . . but you know it's an impact whether or not you notice it or not."

From Study #3 a student said, "I became more accepting of others' beliefs and stopped thinking everyone else was wrong and so going to hell except us in our church."

Given the above data from Catholic students, Catholic teachers, and non-Catholic students, this researcher has concluded the faith and religion of these groups have been affected by the phenomenon of inclusion.

It seems clear that the issue of inclusion deserves close attention not only at the academic and upper administrative levels of Catholic education but also on the front line of Catholic education, the Catholic school, where it is the school principal "as faith leader [who] is the key to this growing accountability for schools to be demonstrably Catholic" (Wallace, 2000, p. 201; see also Ciriello, 1996).

CHAPTER ELEVEN

INCLUSION: A WAY FORWARD

The ten dimensions of inclusion pose both internal and external challenges to Canada's constitutionally protected Catholic schools and although some issues are jurisdictionally dependent, to Catholic schools elsewhere. In addressing those challenges, this Chapter is in two Parts. Part I states the internal challenges and addresses them from the perspective of the Catholic school. Part II summarizes the external challenges and offers reasoned responses to the same.

PART I

The Internal Challenges Posed By Inclusion

The internal challenges posed by inclusion are related to seven of the dimensions mentioned in this book: socio-cultural, racial, administrative, pedagogical, psychological, spiritual, and philosophical. The challenges which follow are presented in aggregate from those dimensions and not specifically related to a specific dimension.

The Challenges

In broad terms, the non-Catholic student participants in Studies 3 and 4 rightly expected that they would be treated as were Catholic students with respect to academic and administrative matters. This is in concert with the expectations of the Catholic school administrators in Study # 2. However, in matters of discipline with respect to areas associated with or directly connected to denominational aspects of the Catholic school, the following areas of conflict arose: in a few cases un-churched non-Catholic students were antagonistic to any religious discussion or instruction; in other cases deeply religious Evangelical families' beliefs in a single source of religious understanding, Holy Scripture, resulted in conflicting Christian messages to students (Raddell, 2000, p. 109); compulsory attendance of non-Catholic students at the school's liturgical services; compulsory attendance of non-Catholic students at the Mass and the Sacrament of Reconciliation; the prohibition of non-Catholic students receiving the Holy Eucharist during the celebration of the Mass at the school; and the requirement that non-Catholic students must attend Catholic religion courses.

In the case of un-churched non-Catholic students who have "no common background or any points of departure" with Catholic teachings and who are "openly skeptical" or "antagonistic . . . seeing little value in exploring the spiritual dimension of life . . . . [where] moral concerns may appear to be unrealistic or naïve . . . .(Raddell, 2000, pp. 109–110) there is little that one can do as a teacher except exhibit the Christian life in one's relationship with the student. That does not mean that a Catholic teacher or school administrator should acquiesce to and accept the inevitability of the student not being evangelized into a belief in a deity but rather that in a spirit of freedom of conscience one should only show the way and lead and not proselytize.

In the case of non-Catholic students who came from a deeply religious Evangelical Christian family which accepts only Holy Scripture as the definitive religious truth it seems necessary, particularly at the interview stage when the student seeks admission, to make clear the Catholic belief that truth is known thorough Holy Scripture, the Tradition of the Catholic Church (Bainvel, 1912), and through the teaching office of the Magisterium (Bainvel, 1912).

Interestingly, in the majority of cases examined by this researcher, none of the above challenges arose with non-Catholic students where (other than in the case of Evangelical fundamentalists Christian families) there was a strong sense of religious commitment to a faith. Indeed, such students expressed support for their Catholic school and its religious program. In particular, the latter students felt empowered in being able to freely express in religious classes, their own belief in God – an action which was generally believed by them as not being acceptable in public school or politically correct within the normal public school adolescent peer group sub-culture.

All of the above challenges may arguably be connected with the non-Catholic student's rights of freedom of religion, freedom of conscience, and the right to be treated with respect as the Other by the institution. How the institution might address these matters follows hereafter.

The Responses

As stated above, there appears to be, in some cases, difficulties with what constitutes the source or sources of religious truth as understood by Catholic school teachers and some non-Catholic students and their families – in particular the Evangelical Christian families. Some non-Catholic students believe that the only authoritative source of religious truth is Holy Scripture. This is not in concert with the Catholic belief that although Sacred Scripture is crucial to the faith, religious truth is also partially understood through the Tradition of the Catholic Church and the teachings of the Magisterium (Raddell, 2000, p. 109). Where there is a challenge by a non-Catholic student to the Catholic belief, such is arguably best resolved through honest and sincere dialogue and considering the challenge as a teachable moment. This matter should be addressed at the initial interview when the non-Catholic student's family approaches the Catholic school for admission of their child.

The challenge faced by a non-Catholic student who is antagonistic to any religious beliefs may be viewed as pastoral matter but it is also certainly an administrative – behavioral – discipline matter as well. It is not sufficient to accept a continuously disruptive presence within the Catholic school given the school's responsibility to all of its students to provide a safe, nurturing, supportive faith and sacramental community. Certainly the disruptive students' freedom to choose to be elsewhere should be respected by the school. However, where the non-Catholic student's family is prepared to proactively assist the school administration and teachers in an attempt to teach the student respect for the school's faith and sacramental community the student should be allowed to continue in the school. In the case where there is not familial support for behavioral change the student should be counseled to move from the school.

The remaining issues are related to compulsory attendance in denominational areas and restrictions on full sacramental participation. In the past, it was believed that non-Catholic students should be exempt from attending religion classes as the latter focused upon orthodoxy which presupposed that the student had been evangelized into the Catholic Faith – which did not apply to the non-Catholic student (Hawker, 1982, p. 28). That view changed with John Paul II's Apostolic Exhortation, "On Catechesis In Our Time" (1979). John Paul II made clear that evangelization need not precede catechesis. Indeed, catechesis (Scannell, 1909) could engender evangelization. However, at least in one instance there was evidence that having separate religion courses for Catholic and non-Catholic students in a Catholic school can be beneficial to both classes of students and for the school (Foley, Pollock, & Walker, 1981).

After interviewing non-Catholic students in Studies 3 and 4, this researcher finds that although catechesis and evangelization are interrelated and the latter may be engendered by the former, there remain compelling social and psychological reasons for the Catholic school exempting non-Catholic students from religion classes which are based upon Catholic orthodoxy. In particular, to compel non-Catholic students to attend such courses can create a pool of resentment within some non-Catholic students which – if not present during their school years – can surface after graduation. It is suggested that if non-Catholic students had the choice to attend Catholic religion classes or generic religion classes such could go a long way to alleviate some of the non-Catholic students' cause célèbre in claiming a lack of freedom of conscience and religion within the Catholic school. Moreover, it seems unreasonable and disingenuous for Catholic schools administrators to require that non-Catholic students attend Catholic sacramental services in the school but only as part participants as the sacraments may not be fully experienced, such as the Eucharist and Reconciliation, by such students. One could say attendance would not hurt non-Catholic students but the evidence – albeit anecdotal and scant – suggests otherwise in that a lingering resentment may be engendered.

Being compelled to attend a dinner but being only offered the appetizer while everyone else dines fully does not engender thankfulness or foster inclusivity of the Other. It should be noted that the researcher seems to be alone in this belief as this position is not supported in any peer-reviewed academic literature which deals with Catholic education known to him. Nevertheless, the issue is important as what is at stake is the non-Catholic students' freedom of religion, freedom of conscience, and a matter of being treated with respect by Catholic teachers and school administrators. To be fair, these students are at least in part correct and in the process of challenging authority and expressing fundamental democratic principles in a free state.

In order to provide some administrative suggestions with respect to the above challenges what follows is information with respect to the three stages of contact between the non-Catholic student and the Catholic school administration: Application for Admission and Post- Admission.

Application for Admission

The role of the Catholic school administrator in her or his relationship with non-Catholic students is as with Catholic students and hence "cannot be reduced to a series of tasks or attitudes. . . It is rather a rich and complex undertaking that defies easy description . . . [with] many personal qualities [being evident] . . . humility, openness, compassion, trust in others, a deep sense of service and dedication (Ontario Conference of Catholic Bishops, 1993, p. 3). There are many administrative approaches (Palestini, 2004) and there are unique challenges. It is true that the school must respect the non-Catholic students' freedom of religion and freedom of conscience, and appreciate the sense of being the Other which has been alluded to in this book. It is also true that in the spirit of ecumenism, and by exploring the Spirit of Assisi (John Paul II, 1986) in the welcoming of the Other to the school's faith community as an integral part of that community, the pastoral approach is experienced by the non-Catholic student. However, in honesty and frankness, the Catholic school must also make clear that the Catholic school is not just a faith community – but a sacramental community which rests its mission within the Catholic church which speaks truth through the Magisterium, the Sacred Scriptures, and the Tradition of the Faith. Orthodoxy (Callan, 1911) is as important as orthopraxis. Hence, the Catholic school can no more accept syncretism (Löffler, 1912), religious relativism (Walker, 1911), nihilism (Palmieri, 1911), a false anthropology (Statement of Conclusions, 1998, para 6), and false Christology (Statement of Conclusions, 1998, para 5) than can the Catholic Church. As an aside, it is important to note that the sharing of religious beliefs within the Catholic school is not syncretism (Zenit, 2007, 06 -18)

Beyond the standard administrative issues of past school records, health records, etc., there are several matters to be addressed at this first contact stage. The research evidences that non-Catholic students are most comfortable if the religious nature of the in-school liturgical services are explained to them upon admission. Often, at least in the experiences of the non-Catholic participants in Studies # 3 and # 4, no explanation on these matters was provided and it is unclear how the non-Catholic student is expected to receive such information. Therefore, it is best that such information is provided during this phase as it is crucial in the determination of whether or not a student and her or his family understands the nature of the Catholic school as an instrument of the Catholic Church. Indeed, as the Congregation for Catholic Education (1988) states,

> The Catholic school is one of these pastoral instruments [of the Catholic Church]; its specific pastoral service consists in mediating between faith and culture: being faithful to the newness of the Gospel while at the same

> time respecting the autonomy and the methods proper to human knowledge. (para. 31)

The Congregation (1988) goes on to say,

> the Catholic school has had a clear identity, not only as a presence of the Church in society, but also as a genuine and proper instrument of the Church. It is a place of evangelization, of authentic apostolate and of pastoral action – not through complementary or parallel or extra-curricular activity, but of its very nature: its work of educating the Christian person (para. 33).

In today's world where even in a Catholic school it may seem that being Christian is primary rather than being Catholic it is important to know that,

> The complexity of the modern world makes it all the more necessary to increase awareness of the ecclesial identity of the Catholic school. It is from its Catholic identity that the school derives its original characteristics and its "structure" as a genuine instrument of the Church, a place of real and specific pastoral ministry. (Congregation, 1997, para. 11)

Indeed, the Catholic school has an "ecclesial nature . . . written in the very heart of its identity as a teaching institution" (para 10). As the Congregation (1997) states further,

> it must be strongly emphasized that this ecclesial dimension [of the Catholic school] is not a mere adjunct, but is a proper and specific attribute, a distinctive characteristic which penetrates and informs every moment of its educational activity, a fundamental part of its very identity and the focus of its mission (para. 12). The fostering of this dimension should be the aim of all those who make up the educating community. (para. 11)

As earlier stated at the Application stage, non-Catholic parents and students should be made aware that the religious truths in Catholicism are based upon tripartite nature of Holy Scripture, Tradition, and the Magisterium in the Catholic faith and further that the school community is not just a faith community but a sacramental community and an entity of the Catholic Church.

At the Application phase, the non-Catholic parents and students should be made aware that the student agrees to attend religion courses and church and liturgical services with the rest of the student body. In that sense, the student is asked to agree to not exercise his or her rights under the Canadian Charter of Rights and Freedoms, in particular the right to freedom of expression and freedom of religion where such would bring disorder to the classroom, and the operation of the Catholic school.

This researcher's research indicates that the singular most important question to be asked of the non-Catholic student's parents on the school's application form is the level of that family's commitment and involvement with their own religion. The level of the non-Catholic family's commitment to its own religion appears to be the singular most important indicator of the success of the Catholic school in being a blessing rather than a burden to the non-Catholic student.

A further point related to the application phase is that for non-religious reasons – that is the Catholic school is closer to the non-Catholic parents' home – the application should be rejected. The application form should clearly ask the reasons for the parents' desire to enroll their children in the Catholic school.

In summation, in the Application phase the following is recommended:

- Informative Statement of Tradition, Scripture, Magisterium, Faith.
- Explanation of terminology: Community, Sacramental Community.
- Quid Pro Quo for Admission: Student's ongoing commitment and acceptance.
- Parental reason for application must be to enter a faith community without which no other reasons will suffice for admission.
- Non-Catholic Parents must be committed as practitioners of their own faith.
- Space must be available in the school's classrooms without over burdening with classroom overload in terms of space and teacher student ratio.
- If special services are required for the non-Catholic student, such services must be already available and offered with space available at the time of admission.
- A written document must be executed by the non-Catholic parents which commits them to the mission of the Catholic school and states that they understand the above points.
- The non-Catholic high school student must sign an assent form which states that she or he understands the Catholic school mission and agrees to abide by the school norms and expectations.

Interestingly the above does not entirely comport with the recommendations of Hawker, (1982, p. 30) where he suggests that Catholic school policies reflect the following:

- The Catholic school participates in the evangelical and educational mission of the Church.
- All parents should understand and accept the purpose, goals, and objectives of the Catholic school.
- All students who attend the Catholic school should be expected to participate in religion class.
- All non-Catholic students who attend the catholic school should be encouraged to participate in the liturgical and para-liturgical programs within the school to the extent that they are able.
- All students who attend the Catholic school are expected to participate in programs of service that are sponsored by the school.

Post-Admission

Following admission there should be continuous attention to the non-Catholic students in the Catholic school. It is unreasonable to expect from school administration that this would be a daily, weekly, or monthly attention. However, at least once a year the non-Catholic student and her or his family should be contacted by the school administration in an attempt to ascertain how the student is faring with respect to the denominational expectations of teachers and administrators in the school. In the event that the number of non-Catholic students makes this task too onerous for administration, then a survey could be employed with a select number of interviews in order to ascertain a general idea of the state of the matter – within the school.

As mentioned earlier, after admission, the non-Catholic student should have the option of attending Catholic religion classes or a special course which is generic in its approach to religion and faith. It appears that this is the case in St. Dominic's Institute of Rome which is "a school which has 400 pupils, including Muslims and nonbelievers from 50 countries" (Zenit, February 10, 2006). This approach would allow for the exploration of faith and religions and hence evangelization while preserving the students' freedom of religion and conscience. Certainly, if a non-Catholic student decided to attend Catholic religious classes she or he would be invited to share her or his family's beliefs in the Spirit of Assisi and ecumenism (Steinwachs, 1994).

All students in the school would be expected to actively participate in quasi-religious activities such as those involving matters of Social Justice required in either the Catholic or non-Catholic religion courses.

All students would be invited to attend the sacramental services, the Eucharist and Reconciliation, within the school but the non-Catholic students would not be compelled to do so. Alternative activities would be offered to those non-participants. All students would be required to attend non-sacramental religious services within the school and asked to fully participate in matters such as reading Sacred Scripture to those congregated for the service. Non-Christian students would also be encouraged to participate in such services and, again in the Spirit of Assisi, to share their faith where appropriate in the circumstances.

It is significant that the Catholic Church has spoken of ecumenism (Vatican II, 1964b, Nov. 21) and it is also significant that as the number of non-Catholic students has increased since the Vatican II document Unitatis Redintegratio (Decree On Ecumenism).

Now seems the time to address ecumenism in applicable terms of the Catholic school. This was emphasized by Steinwachs (1994) when she suggested that Catholic schools "move forward the cause of ecumenism" and suggested the following, among other things (p. 53):

- Review the school philosophy and ask if it mentioned ecumenism;
- Plan a few school prayer services which flow from "Hebrew Scripture";
- Open dialogue amongst parents, teachers and students regarding ecumenism and speak of that topic at one staff meeting a year;
- Establish a school goal "to appreciate the dignity of each individual";
- Make prayer evident in the school;
- "Encourage teachers and students to study the church's documents on ecumenism"
- "Offer course work on other faiths . . . stress those elements which unite us"; and
- Offer a strong course on Catholicism to all students.

In the Catholic school the above is possible only if the Catholic school administrators and Catholic teachers open their hearts and minds to the needs of non-Catholic students and accept that those needs must be addressed after admission.

The unique nature of the Catholic school administrator is stated hereafter and explains that for her or him the way of living the role is as important as the decisions made.

> on a daily basis they struggle to deal with a complex constellation of contentious realities. Their unenviable, but vital task is to meet these challenges in a way that contributes to the nature, mission and culture of their school. Catholicity demands that not only the outcomes but the very processes by which they are achieved embody the gospel values. The creation of a genuine Catholic school culture lies in the synthesis of response and result (Roche, 1996, p. 46) .

The above reflects what the Congregation for Catholic Education (1988) sees as what makes a Catholic school unique. It said,

> While the Catholic school is like any other school in this complex variety of events that make up the life of the school, there is one essential difference: it draws its inspiration and its strength from the Gospel in which it is rooted. The principle that no human act is morally indifferent to one's conscience or before God has clear applications to school life: examples of it are school work accepted as a duty and done with good will; courage and perseverance when difficulties come; respect for teachers; loyalty toward and love for fellow students; sincerity, tolerance, and goodness in all relationships. (para. 47)

In relationship with the non-Catholic student, Catholic school administrators and teachers should exhibit in their praxis the Gifts of the Holy Spirit: charity, faith, prudence, fortitude, faith, justice, and hope which according to St. Thomas Aquinas (1948, First Part of the Second Part Q. 68) correspond to the seven Capital Virtues of wisdom, knowledge, counsel, fortitude, understanding, piety, and fear f the Lord. A particularly useful book which is helpful in explaining the Catholic school principal's role as a spiritual leader within the Catholic school has been published by the United States Catholic Conference, and edited by Maria J. Ciriello, entitled, "Formation and Development for Catholic School Leaders: Volume II – The Principal as Spiritual Leader" (1996).

In summary, Catholic school administrators and Catholic teachers should consider the principles of evangelization, the Spirit of Assisi, ecumenism, and the spiritual nature of their vocation as stated in Lay Catholics Witnesses to Faith (Congregation, 1982) on their ongoing relationship with non-Catholic students. In particular, school officials and teachers must ensure that thee non-Catholic student's freedom of religion and freedom of conscience is respected and protected within the institution of Catholic education.

PART II

The External Challenges Posed By Inclusion

The external challenges raised by inclusion relate to law, finance, and politics. The legal challenges deal with constitutional issues. The financial challenges are closely intertwined with the political challenges and hence will be addressed jointly.

The Legal Challenges and Responses

These challenges are concerned with maintaining the constitutionally protected rights of Catholic schools in the Provinces of Ontario, Alberta, and Saskatchewan as well protecting the denominational aspects of Catholic schools funded by those three provinces notwithstanding federal and provincial human rights guarantees for all teachers and students. Because Catholic schools in these provinces are constitutionally protected and receive public funds by right, albeit also in part by compromise as in Ontario for Grades 9 to 12 and in Saskatchewan in Grades 9 to 12, rather than as private schools through privilege, they must be concerned with the protection of those rights as they could be abrogated constitutionally through a provincial referendum followed by an Act of the provincial legislature and a subsequent Act of Parliament – as was the case in Quebec and in Newfoundland-Labrador. The core defense for Catholic schools which face this challenge is not legal but rather political and will be addressed under that topic hereafter. The second legal issue facing Catholic schools also deals with the constitutional issues surrounding the Canadian Charter of Rights and Freedoms and provincial human rights legislation. In situations where non-Catholic parents challenge legislation so that they may become members of the catholic school board as is the case in the North West Territories, or where a non-Catholic students claims to seek refuge behind the Catholic concept of conscience understood as the "Restless hear towards God," it becomes incumbent upon Catholic school boards to demand the protection of the rights of Catholic schools in an area comprising the province in question before the geographical area in which they are found entered confederation and to stand facts to the teachings of the Magisterium. However, the procedure with which schools enforce the teachings of the Magisterium will be subject to judicial scrutiny and hence the rules of natural justice and procedural fairness must be abided by in such circumstances. Moreover, Catholic schools must ensure that the denominational norms which are being sought to be enforced within the school when a breach occurs by a non-Catholic students is dealt with in a consistent and pastoral fashion which takes into account the particular religious beliefs of the student's religion without compromising the religious and spiritual nature of the Catholic school faith community.

The Financial and Political Challenges and Responses

There is not yet a serious challenge to the public financing of Catholic schools in Ontario, Alberta, and Saskatchewan in so far as inclusion is concerned. However, the overarching question for such schools is "why should society support with public funds two systems of education? Does such institutional dualism result in a duplication of services and capital costs such that there is inherently wastage?" The researcher is not aware of any authoritative studies on this issue; therefore, it is unknown if this indeed correct. However, in one jurisdiction, the City of Calgary, Alberta, the local bishop, Bishop Henry (personal communication, August, 2003), has stated that his examination of the issue indicates that there is no extra costs involved in having a dual system of public and separate schools in the province of Alberta (See also Gonzalez, 2002, Nov. 4).

The political challenges related to inclusion involve the duplication of financial expenditures argument stated above, the anti-democratic sentiment which is alleged to be involved with separate schools for Catholics and ghettoization for those students, the alleged poaching of non-Catholic students by Catholic schools to enhance the expansion and financial aspects of the Catholic schools, and the challenge by other religious groups to the exclusive right of Catholic separate schools to funding by the governments of Ontario, Alberta, and Saskatchewan due to what some consider an historical context which no longer exists in Canadian society. Clearly these arguments, or at least some of them, contributed to the end of constitutionally protected Catholic schools in the Provinces of Quebec (Canada: Privy Council Office, 1997), and Newfoundland-Labrador (Constitutional Amendment Proclamation, 1997; see also CBC News, "Newfoundland votes for secular schools," 1997).

There has been some anecdotal evidence that some poaching of non-Catholic students has occurred in a few cases in a few schools but there is no evidence that poaching has ever been a formal or informal policy of any Canadian Catholic school division or system. As Catholic are in a minority in Ontario, Alberta, and Saskatchewan it would be unethical, and politically foolish, to engage in such an activity when it is through the good will of the body politic that the rights of Catholic schools are maintained within each province. Catholic schools in those three provinces already face difficulties with some groups in their provinces who would not be sorry to see the demise of constitutionally protected Catholic schools.

The defense of constitutionally protected Catholic schools could be focused upon the following arguments: such religiously protected schools offer a theistic values education to those of many faiths – not just Christians – who are more comfortable sending their children to such schools for no cost above what it costs top send their children to the public school systems. For many immigrants of a deep faith, a private school's costs are prohibitive. Moreover, the common good of Canadian society is enriched by such schools in the manner of acceptance of the Other and treatment of those of difference as stated earlier in this book. The arguments seem persuasive from both liberal and communitarian perspectives. These are the arguments which must be employed to defend the existence of constitutionally protected Catholic schools in the public square in Canadian society.

APPENDIX A

Study # 2

[SCHOOL] BOARD REGULATION: THE ADMISSION OF NON-CATHOLIC STUDENTS

Background

Our schools exist in order to serve the educational needs of the residents of the jurisdiction. We have a mandate in legislation to offer the program of studies prescribed by [the Province] and the mandate to do so within the context of the Catholic Church's mission to educate the whole person in the name of Jesus Christ.

The XXX Act of [Province] recognizes . . . . [the] primary mandate is to provide education programs to students through . . . the public school and the separate schools.

The Board stipulates that this education must be based on the Catholic concept of the human person and that the objectives and purposes of education . . . must be set in this total Christian concept.

The Congregation for Catholic Education (1988) declared the distinctiveness of the Catholic school in its religious dimension, and that this is to be found in the educational climate, the personal development of each student, the relationship established between culture and the Gospel and the illumination of all knowledge with the light of faith.

The documents of Vatican II state that, as Catholics, we are called to unity with all believers. We are invited by out Church's teaching to respond to the concept of ecumenism and to appreciate the giftedness of other religious traditions.

The Board recognizes that many parents of the pluralistic believing community, some of whom are not of the Catholic faith, are seeking an education that includes the spiritual and moral, as well as the cognitive, social, and physical domains.

Desired Outcome/s

That given adequate resources, facilities and programs, the division welcomes students whose parents or guardians wish them: to participate in the academic, social, physical and religious education program offered in the division's schools;

to be educated in the context of the Catholic community, which is a sign of the reign of God as revealed by Jesus Christ; and, to receive all the benefits and assume all the responsibilities of membership associated with membership in the Catholic school community. The same welcome is extended to independent students seeking the same educational benefits.

That our staff is guided by the following statement from the sacred Congregation for catholic Education when working with non-Catholic students:

"Not all students in Catholic schools are members of the Catholic Church; not all are Christians. There are, in fact, countries in which the vast majority of the students are not Catholics . . . The religious freedom and the personal conscience of individual students ands their families must be respected, and this freedom is explicitly recognized by the Church. On the other hand, a Catholic school cannot relinquish its won freedom to proclaim the Gospel and to offer a formation based on the values to be found in a Christian education; this is its right and its duty. To proclaim or to offer is not to impose, however; the latter suggests a moral violence which is strictly forbidden, both by the Gospel and by Church law."

Procedures

1. Parents/guardians of non-resident students wishing to enroll their child(ren) in any school in the decision must make a request to the respective principal.

2. The principal shall begin the decision-making process to admit the applicant dependent on sufficient resources, facilities and programs in the school after all resident students (current and projected) have been housed and an appropriate program is available. This is to be interpreted as including space in special education programs as well. The principal shall consider classroom particulars, class size, physical space and other factors as appropriate to determine sufficient resources, facilities and programs.

3. If, in the opinion of the school principal, the above conditions have been met, the principal shall convene a meeting of the parents/guardians and if the student is ten years of age or older, the student to explain: the board's vision, mission, fundamental beliefs and characteristics of a Christian community; the expectations that all students receive religious education instruction and participate in faith-based activities including "good works" projects; the nature and frequency of religious celebrations; the special role of the Sacraments; the outward manifestations of our Catholic faith; the involvement of all students in regular prayer; the respect and tolerance we show to other faiths,; ways in which the Catholic faith differs from other Christian denominations; and the fact that we expect non-Catholic students and their parents/guardians to respect t and accept the Catholic character of our schools. The principal will also explain the context of the non-Catholic registration form. The same procedures shall hold in the case of an independent student.

4. Applicants will be made fully aware of the nature and philosophy of a catholic school prior to freely choosing to become a member of the school community; and applicants who later choose not to honor their responsibilities as members of the Catholic school community may withdraw their child(ren).

5. If the school principal feels that the parents/guardians ands student understand and accept the Catholic nature of the school, the principal shall review the records of all such students to establish their suitability for admission. If the principal fees that the student's academic needs can be met by the school, the principal may sign-off on the application for the non-Catholic students. At this point the student is accepted into the school.

6. The principal shall have the remainder of the appropriate admission forms completed and they shall become part of the student's cumulative record.

REFERENCES

[Relevant Provincial Act]
The Religious Dimension of Education in a Catholic School, a document of the Sacred Congregation for Catholic Education, Rome, 1988. The Canadian Conference of Catholic Bishops Publications, Ottawa, Ont.

APPENDIX B

Study # 2

ENTRANCE FORM FOR NON-CATHOLICS

Entrance Interview Questions

Family Name ____________________________

Parent's Names ________________________, ____________________________

1. Child's Name _____________________, Sex _____ Age _____ Grade _____

School they are attending now _______________________________

2. Child's Name _____________________, Sex _____ Age _____ Grade _____

School they are attending now _______________________________

3. Child's Name _____________________, Sex _____ Age _____ Grade _____

School they are attending now _______________________________

4. Child's Name _____________________, Sex _____ Age _____ Grade _____

School they are attending now _______________________________

What are the reasons you choosing XXXXXX School for your child's education?

How are you willing to contribute to help in your child's education? What strengths and/or talents do you as parent(s) have that you can contribute to the school?

If your child is experiencing difficulties at school, are you willing to work, in full cooperation, with the teachers, administration and support staff to assist your child to get the best education they can? (e.g. Resource, Early Intervention, family resource)

APPENDIX B

XXXX is a Catholic school. We are overt in our Faith and it permeates all that we do. This includes the curriculum, religion classes, morning exercises, extra curricular activities and discipline. Do you have any concerns with your child being exposed to the teachings of the church and the teachings of the gospel? Would these teachings be in anyway contradictory to your religious denomination?

Do you have objections to your child:

Participating in prayer ______
Praying the rosary (Hail Mary) _____
Participating in religious celebrations, liturgies and masses _____
Participating in Ash Wednesday Celebration? _____
Respecting the values and practices of our faith? _____

Are you aware of any special provisions or health issues that the school needs to be aware of?

9. Do you foresee your child having challenges that the school needs to be aware of? (Behavior, speech, listening). Has your child been screened for any of these or other issues?

Please sign below that we have had an interview on the date sign:

_______________________________ _______________________________
Parents Signature Principal's Signature

____
Date

APPENDIX C

Study # 2

QUESTIONS POSED TO CATHOLIC SCHOOL ADMINISTRATORS

1. What are the current district and school policies related to the admission of non-Catholic students?
2. What are the current district and school policies related to the continued presence of non-Catholic students?
3. What is your understanding of the raison d'etre for the above policies?
4. In your experience, how well do those policies achieve their administrative purposes within your school?

Please tell me abut your school:

(1) The socio-economic area and population it serves,
(2) Is it Urban or Rural or a mix?
(3) How many students in total?
(4) How many non-Catholic students?
(5) What is the mix of Christian to non-Christian?
(6) How involved in the school are the parents of non-Catholic students?
(7) Although there is a school district policy how does the admission process for non-Catholic students work out in practice?
(8) Of what significance, if any, is the non-Catholic family's commitment to their faith with regard to admission of their child to your school?
(9) What is asked of the non-Catholic family after their child has been admitted to your school?
(10) What religious studies program is used in your school?
(11) How do you react as an administrator when a non-Catholic student breaches a denominational norm or religious expectation of your Catholic school?
(12) Are there any special programs for non-Catholic students?
(13) Have you brought the school district policy to the attention of your staff? When -at the beginning of each year?
(14) Do you think that the number of non-Catholic students in your school is significant? If so, in what ways and to whom?

APPENDIX D

Study # 3

QUESTIONS POSED TO GRADUATED NON-CATHOLIC STUDENTS

I. Interview Questions

1. When you hear the words, "Catholic education" what picture or pictures come to your mind?
2. The word community can mean many things. What does that word mean to you?
3. Think back on your relationships and conversations with your Catholic friends in your school. How was faith (religion) expressed in those conversations?
4. You have attended many classes with Catholic students. In what ways were having Catholic students in your classes interesting?
5. During the school year, the teachers and students, including Catholic students, gather for mass and school liturgies. What are your feelings about these gatherings?
6. During your high school years, you have made friends, acquaintances and come to know your teachers. You have been part of that school group or community. How would you describe the relationships in that community?
7. How were you welcomed into your school?

II Ending Question

1. Overall, what are the most important things to you about attending a Catholic high school?

III Summary Questions

1. Is there anything we should have talked about but did not?
2. Have we missed anything?
3. Is this an adequate summary?

IV Closing Statement

Thank you very much for participating in this research study.

APPENDIX E

ENTRANCE FORM AND POLICY STATEMENTS FOR NON-CATHOLICS

Entrance Interview Questions

Family Name_____________________________

Parent's Names ___________________________,
____

1. Child's Name ______________________, Sex _____ Age _____ Grade _____

School they are attending now _________________________________

2. Child's Name ______________________, Sex _____ Age _____ Grade _____

School they are attending now _________________________________

3. Child's Name ______________________, Sex _____ Age _____ Grade _____

School they are attending now _________________________________

4. Child's Name ______________________, Sex _____ Age _____ Grade _____

School they are attending now _________________________________

What are the reasons you choosing XXXXXX School for your child's education?

How are you willing to contribute to help in your child's education? What strengths and/or talents do you as parent(s) have that you can contribute to the school?

If your child is experiencing difficulties at school, are you willing to work, in full cooperation, with the teachers, administration and support staff to assist your child to get the best education they can? (e.g. Resource, Early Intervention, family resource)

XXXX is a Catholic school. We are overt in our Faith and it permeates all that we do. This includes the curriculum, religion classes, morning exercises, extra curricular activities and discipline. Do you have any concerns with your child being exposed to the teachings of the church and the teachings of the gospel? Would these teachings be in anyway contradictory to your religious denomination?

Do you have objections to your child:

Participating in prayer ______
Praying the rosary (Hail Mary) _____
Participating in religious celebrations, liturgies and masses _____
Participating in Ash Wednesday Celebration? _____
Respecting the values and practices of our faith? _____

Are you aware of any special provisions or health issues that the school needs to be aware of?

9. Do you foresee your child having challenges that the school needs to be aware of? (Behavior, speech, listening). Has your child been screened for any of these or other issues?

Please sign below that we have had an interview on the date sign:

________________________________ ________________________________

Parents Signature Principal's Signature

____

Date

NOTES

[1] This comment by the court displays a misunderstanding of the nature of Catholic education and equates the latter with a secular education. The gathering was a celebration of the completion of many years within a Catholic institution which focuses upon the faith community, faith development, permeation of the morality of the Catholic Faith in all events, and indeed the evangelization of Catholic youth. It was not a public event as either one had to be a student of the Catholic school or be invited by a Catholic student. It was not a gathering of youth at a rock concert or a party after a public athletic event.

[2] 15. (1) Every individual is equal before and under the law and has the right to the equal protection and equal benefit of the law without discrimination and, in particular, without discrimination based on race, national or ethnic origin, colour, religion, sex, age or mental or physical disability.

[3] Oxaal (2003) reviews the legal test for issuing an injunction. For the purposes of this paper it is sufficient to know that there must be a sense of urgency to the application, in the sense that to wait for trial would make the right sought moot as the crucial moment would have passed.

[4] Mr. Hall actually had a much stronger case to be made as the Supreme Court of Canada has opted to support "negative liberty" when and individual's liberties are restricted by an administrative body.

[5] Mr. Justice MacKinnon suggested that in *Hall* the discrimination was actual not hypothetical as in *Trinity*. That is correct. However, in *Trinity* the issue was not denominational breach by an individual claiming membership within the denominational institution and who ostensibly ascribed to its precepts of behavior. See Donlevy (2003c); see also Donlevy (2005).

[6] The issue of how this argument might be viewed by the court if a non-Catholic student were involved, is currently being researched by this author. However, for an interesting paper on the rights of non-Catholic students in Catholic schools see Donlevy (2005). For a commentary on how Catholic students perceive non-Catholic students and the effect of the latter on the former see Donlevy (2003a).

[7] Author's note: Aquinas's lecture notes entitled, "Disputed Questions on the Truth" have been translated in part by Potts. That translation is contained in Potts' 1980 book. All subsequent quotations from Aquinas from Disputed Questions on the Truth are from Potts' translation and are referenced to the pages in Potts' book.

REFERENCES

Ackernam, B. (1990). Neutralities. In R. B. Douglass, G. M. Mara, & H. S. Richardson (Eds.), *Liberalism and the good* (pp. 29–43). New York: Routledge.

Adler v. Ontario, 3 S.C.R. 609. (1996). 140 D.L.R. (4th) 385 (S.C.C.). Retrieved March 5, 2009 from http://www.canlii.org/en/ca/scc/doc/1996/1996canlii148/1996canlii148.html

Apuleius. (1984). *On the god of Socrates* (T. Taylor, Trans.). Sequim, WA: Holmes Publishing Group.

Aquinas, T. (1948). *Summa theologica* (Complete English Edition in Five Volumes) (Fathers of the English Dominican Province, Trans., Vol. One-Two). Allen, TX: Christian Classics: A Division of Thomas More Publishing. (Original Publication Date: 1274) Retrieved March 5, 2009 from http://www.newadvent.org/summa/

Aristotle. (350 B.C.E). *Nicomachaen ethics*. Retrieved March 5, 2007, from http://classics.mit.edu/Aristotle/nicomachaen.html

Aumann, J. (1985). Christian Spirituality in the Catholic Tradition. Ft. Collins, CO.; Ignatius Press

Bainvel, J. (1912). Tradition and living Magisterium. In *The Catholic encyclopedia* (Vol. XV). New York: Robert Appleton Company. Retrieved April 13, 2009 from New Advent: http://www.newadvent.org/cathen/15006b.htm

Baker v. Canada (Minister of Citizenship and Immigration). (1999). 2 Supreme Court of Canada Reports. 817. Retrieved March 5, 2009 from http://www.canlii.org/en/ca/scc/doc/1999/1999canlii699/1999canlii699.html

Beck, L. C., Trombetta, W. L., & Share, S. (1986). Using focus group sessions before decisions are made. *North Carolina Medical Journal, 47*(2).

Bellah, R. N. (1998). Community properly understood: A defense of democratic communitarianism. In A. Etzioni (Ed.), *The essential communitarian reader* (pp. 15–20). Lanham, MD: Rowman and Littlefield.

Benedict XVI. (2006, September 4). *Pope notes conditions for interreligious prayer meetings*. Retrieved January 4, 2007, from http://www.zenit.org/article-16879?l=english

Bentham, J. (1996). *An introduction to the principles of morals and legislation* (J. H. Burns & H. L. A. Hart, Eds.). Oxford: Clarendon Press.

Berlin, I. (1959). *The crooked timber of humanity*. New York: Alfred A. Knopf, Inc.

Berlin, I. (2002). Two concepts of liberty. In H. Hardy (Ed.), *Liberty* (pp. 166–217). Oxford: Oxford University Press. (Original work published 1958)

Benson, I. T. (1999–2000). *Notes towards a (Re)definition of the "Secular"*. University of British Columbia Law Review. pp. 519- 549 Retrieved March 5, 2009 from http://culturalrenewal.ca/downloads/sb_culturalrenewal/benson050405.pdf

Bishops of NSW and the ACT (2007, August). *Catholic Schools at a Crossroads, Pastoral Letter of the Bishops of NSW and the ACT*. Retrieved March 6, 2009 from http://www.cso.brokenbay.catholic.edu.au/about/news/pdfs/Catholic%20schools%20at%20the%20crossroads.pdf

Boase, S. (2006, May 5). A lesson in diversity. *The Hamilton Spectator*. Retrieved May 3, 2008, from www.hwcdsb.edu.on.ca/news_archives/05_06/mf_na_lesson_diversity.html

Bogle, J. (2007, November 5). inside catholic.com. Retrieved from http://insidecatholic.com/Joomla/index.php?option=com_content&task=view&id=1363&Itemid=121

Board of Trustees of Aspen View Regional Division No. 19 and Sidney Kuryliw v. Attorney General of Alberta and the Minister of Learning for the Province of Alberta. Q.B. Action No. 0403 21814. Judicial District of Edmonton, Alberta.

Boyack, K. (Ed.). (1992). *The new Catholic evangelization*. New Jersey, NJ: Paulist Press.

Buber, M. (2002). *Between man and man* (R. Gregor-Smith, Trans.). New York: Routledge. (Original published 1947)

Burwell, J. S. (2005). *Another experience of the holy: Fostering dialogue about religion and God in Catholic schools with multifaith student populations*. M.Ed. Thesis, University of Manitoba.

Bryk, A. S., Lee, V. E., & Holland, P. B. (1993). *Catholic schools and the common good*. Cambridge, MA: Harvard University Press.

Caldwell, S. (2008). Muslim prayer rooms should be opened in Catholic schools, say church leaders. Mail Online. Retrieved March 5, 2009 from http://www.dailymail.co.uk/news/article-1091218/Muslim-prayer-rooms-opened-Catholic-schools-say-church-leaders.html

Caldwell v. Stewart. (1984), 15 DLR (4th) 1 (SCC). Retrieved March 4, 2009 from http://www.canlii.org/en/ca/scc/doc/1984/1984canlii128/1984canlii128.html

Callan, C. (1911). Orthodoxy. In *The Catholic encyclopedia*. New York: Robert Appleton Company. Retrieved October 26, 2008, from New Advent www.newadvent.org/cathen/11330a.htm

Canada: Privy Council Office. (1997, April 22). Statement by Minister Dion on the Amendment of Section 93 (Education) of the Constitutional Act, 1867. House of Commons, Ottawa, Ontario. Retrieved October 20, 2008, from www.pco-bcp.gc.ca/aia/index.asp?lang=eng&Page=archive&Sub=speeches&Doc=19970422_e.htm

Canada v. Schmidt 1 S.C.R. 500 (1987). Retrieved from http://scc.lexum.umontreal.ca/en/1987/1987rcs1-500/1987rcs1-500.html

Canadian Bill of Rights. S.C. 1960, c. 44. Retrieved October 1, 2007, from www.canlii.org/ca/sta/c-12.3/

Canadian Broadcasting Company. (1999, November 5). *UN says funding of Catholic schools discriminatory*. Retrieved May 3, 2007, from www.cbc.ca/news/story/1999/11/05/schools 991105. html

Canadian Catholic School Trustees‘ Association. (2006, June 9). *St. John's Convention – Panel discussion: Hard, hard, times: The loss of denominational rights in Newfoundland*. Retrieved May 2, 2008, from www.ccsta.ca/news_detail.cfm?id=10

Canadian Catholic School Trustees‘ Association: Quick Notes from Winter Board of Directors‘ Meetings: Highlights of Provincial Reports. (n.d.). Retrieved May 7, 2005, from www.ccsta.ca/quicknotes.htm

Canadian Charter of Rights and Freedoms, Part I of the *Constitution Act, 1982* being Schedule B of the *Canada Act, 1982* (U.K.). (1982). c.11. Retrieved April 8, 2005, from http://laws.justice.gc.ca/en/charter/#garantie

Canadian Civil Liberties Association. (2007, September 24). *National post*. Retrieved May 4, 2008, from www.nationalpost.com/news/story.html?id=18a42b14-3371-4d44-b517-c1170277a231

Canadian Conference of Catholic Bishops. (1990). Born of the Spirit: English Canadian Catechetical Series (Years 1–6). National Office of Religious Education of the Canadian Conference of Catholic Bishops. Ottawa: Publications Service - Canadian Conference of Catholic Bishops. Retrieved May 7, 2006, from www.cccbpublications.ca/miva/merchant.mv?Screen=CTGY&Store_Code=cccb-eng&Category_Code=CAT-BOS

Canadian Conference of Catholic Bishops. (1973). Statement on the Formation of Conscience. Retrieved March 5, 2009 from http://www.consciencelaws.org/Examining-Conscience-Ethical/Ethical40.html

Canadian Conference of Catholic Bishops. (n.d.). *We are strong together*. [Grades 7-10, & 12] National Office of Religious Education of the Canadian Conference of Catholic Bishops. Ottawa: Publications Service - Canadian Conference of Catholic Bishops. Retrieved May 7, 2006, from www.cccbpublications.ca/miva/merchant.mv?Screen=CTGY&Store_Code=cccb-eng&Category_Code=CAT-WST

Carey, B. (2007, March 22). Brain injury said to affect moral choices. *New York Times*. Retrieved March 5, 2009 from http://www.nytimes.com/2007/03/22/science/22brain.html?_r=1&ref=science&oref=slogin

Casagrande v. Hinton (R.C. Separate School District No. 155). (1987). 51 Alta. L. R. (2d) 349 (Q.B.).

Catechism of the Catholic Church. (n.d.) Retrieved March 5, 2005, from www.vatican.va/archive/ccc_css/archive/catechism/ccc_toc.htm

Catholic Civil Rights League. (2007, May 28). Canadian territorial court rules Catholic schools must accept non-Catholic trustees. Retrieved May 1, 2008, from www.ccrl.ca/index.php?id=4854

Catholic News. (2005, April 8). *Non-Catholic cap threatening Catholic school viability*. Retrieved from www.cathnews.com/news/504/49.php

Catholic World News. (2008, January 23). Retrieved from www.catholicculture.org/news/features/ index.cfm?recnum=56147

CBC News. (1997, July 2). *Newfoundland votes for secular schools*. Retrieved October 20, 2008, from http://archives.cbc.ca/society/education/clips/15515/

Chadwick, P. (1994). *Schools of reconciliation: Issues in joint Roman Catholic – Anglican education*. New York: Cassell.

Charmaz, K. (2000). Grounded theory. In N. K. Denzin & Y. S. Lincoln (Eds.), *Handbook of qualitative research* (2nd ed., pp. 509–535). Thousand Oaks, CA: Sage.

Chryssides, G. D. (1999). Buddhism and conscience. In J. Hoose (Ed.), *Conscience in world religions* (pp. 176–199). Notre Dame, IN: University of Notre Dame Press.

Cicero. (1913). *De Officiis, III.vi.26; III, vi 30* (W. Miller, Trans.). Cambridge: Harvard University Press. Retrieved March 5, 2007, from www.constitution.org/rom/de_officiis.htm (Original published 44 B.C.E.)

Ciriello, M. J. (1996). *Formation and development for Catholic school leaders: Volume II – The principal as spiritual leader* (2nd ed.). Washington, DC: Department of Education, United States Catholic Conference.

Congregation for Catholic Education. (1977). The Catholic school. In A. Fllannery (Ed.), The Vatican collection Vatican II, Vol. 2: More post conciliar documents (New Rev. ed., pp. 606–629). Newport, NY: Costello Publishing Company, Inc. Retrieved March 5 2009 from http://www.vatican.va/ roman_curia/congregations /ccatheduc/documents/rc_con_ccatheduc_doc_19770319_ catholic-school_ en.html

Congregation for Catholic Education. (1982). Lay Catholics in schools: Witnesses to faith. In A. Fllannery (Ed.), The Vatican collection, Vatican II, Vol. 2: More post conciliar documents (New Rev. ed., pp. 630–661). Newport, NY: Costello Publishing Company, Inc. Retrieved October 19, 2008, from www.vatican.va/roman_curia/congregations/ccatheduc/ documents/rc_con_ccatheduc_ doc_19821015_lay-catholics_en.html

Congregation for Catholic Education. (1988). *The religious dimension of education in a Catholic school*. Washington, DC: United States Catholic Conference. Retrieved October 20, 2008, from www.vatican.va/roman_curia/congregations/ccatheduc/documents/rc_com_ccatheduc_doc_1988040 7_catholic-school_en.html

Congregation for Catholic Education: For Seminaries and Educational Institutions. (1997). *The Catholic school on the threshold of the third millennium*. Retrieved October 20, 2008, from www.vatican.va/ roman_curia/congregations/ccatheduc/documents/rc_con_ccatheduc_doc_ 27041998_ school2000_ en.. html

Congregation for the Clergy (1997, August 11). General Directory For Catechesis. Retrieved March 4, 2009 from http://www.vatican.va/roman_curia/congregations/ cclergy/documents/rc_con_ccatheduc _doc_17041998_directory-for-catechesis_en.html

Congregation for the Doctrine of the Faith. (1986, October 1). *Letter to the Bishops of the Catholic church on the pastoral care of homosexual persons* (Homosexualitatis problema *Epistula de pastorali personarum homosexualium cura*). Retrieved September 18, 2008, from www.vatican.va/roman_ curia/congregations/cfaith/documents/rc_con_cfaith_doc_19861001_homosexual-persons_ en.html

Congregation for the Doctrine of the Faith. (2000a). *Dominus iesus* (Declaration on the unicity and salvific universality of Jesus Christ and the Church). Boston: Pauline Books and Media. Retrieved October 10, 2008, from www.vatican.va/roman_curia/congregations/cfaith/documents/rc_con_ cfaith_doc_20000806_dominus-iesus_en.html

Congregation for the Doctrine of the Faith. (2000b). *Note on the expression "Sister Churches"*. L'Osservatore Romano (English ed.). Retrieved October 10, 2008, from www.vatican.va/roman_ curia/congregations/cfaith/documents/rc_con_cfaith_doc_20000630_chiese-sorelle_en.html

Constitution Act. (1867). Retrieved October 10, 2005, from http://laws.justice.gc.ca/en/const/ c1867_e. html#provincial

Constitutional Amendment Proclamation, 1997 (Newfoundland Act). (1997, April 21). Retrieved October 20, 2008, from www.canadiana.org/citm/_textpopups/constitution/con_amend_1997_e.html

REFERENCES

Criminal Code of Canada. (n.d.). Retrieved March 6, 2009 from http://laws.justice.gc.ca/en/showtdm/cs/C-46

Cunningham, L.S., & Egan, K.J. (1996). Christian Spirituality: Themes from the Tradition. Mahwah, New Jersey: Paulist Press.

Debuchy, P. (1912). Spiritual exercises of Saint Ignatius. In *The Catholic encyclopedia*. New York: Robert Appleton Company. Retrieved May 31, 2008, from New Advent: www.newadvent.org/cathen/14224b.htm

Delhayne, P. (1968). *The Christian conscience* (C. Quinn, Trans.). New York: Desclee.

Dershowitz, A. M. (1996). Life is not a dramatic narrative. In P. Brooks & P. Gerwitz (Eds.), *Law's stories: Narrative and rhetoric in the law*. New Haven, CT: Yale University Press.

Donlevy, J. K. (2003a). *Catholic education and the inclusion of non-Catholic students: Qualitative findings and implications*. Unpublished Doctoral Dissertation, University of Saskatchewan, Saskatoon, Saskatchewan. Retrieved March 5, 2009 from http://library2.usask.ca/theses/available/etd-09252008-113529/unrestricted/Donlevy_James_Kent_sec_nc._2003.pdf

Donlevy, J. K. (2003b). Catholic schools and open boundaries: The inclusion of non-Catholic students. *Canadian Journal of Education, 27*(1), 101–118.

Donlevy, J. K. (2003c). Canadian education: Who's values? Who's rights (The Trinity Western University Case). *International Electronic Journal for Leadership in Learning, 7*(20). Retrieved May 6, 2005, from www.acs.ucalgary.ca/~iejll/

Donlevy, J. K. (2005). Re-visiting denominational cause and denominational breach in Canada's constitutionally protected Catholic schools. *Journal of Education and Law, 15*(3), 85–112.

Donlevy, J. K. (2006a). History, law, and religion: The school district boundary issue in Alberta. *Journal of Educational Administration and Foundations, 17*(2), 43–72.

Donlevy, J. K. (2006b). Non-Catholic students impact upon Catholic students in four Catholic high schools. *Journal of Religion and Society, 8*. Retrieved from http://moses.creighton.edu/JRS/2006/2006-3.html

Donlevy, J. K. (2007a). Ten dimensions of inclusion: Non-Catholic students in Catholic schools. Catholic education. *A Journal of Inquiry and Practice, 11*(1), 293–320.

Donlevy, J. K. (2007b). Non-Catholic students impact on Catholic teachers in four Catholic high schools religious education. *Journal of Religion and Society, 102*(1), 4–24.

Donlevy, J. K. (2008a). Non-Catholic students' experiences in a Catholic high school: Two qualitative studies. *Journal of Religious Education (Australia)* 56(*4*), 29-39.

Donlevy, J. K. (2008b). The Common Good: Catholic Schools and the Inclusion of non-Catholic Students. *Journal of Beliefs and Values: Studies in Religion and Education* .Vol. 29, No. 2, pp. 161-171. [United Kingdom.]

Donlevy, J.K. (2008c). Catholic Schools and Freedom of Conscience in the Canadian Charter of Rights and Freedoms *Journal of Catholic Legal Studies* (St. John's School of Law, New York). Symposium Issue Vol. 47, 1, pp. 69-96.

Dixon, R. (2003, November 9). Catholic schools caught in a bind. *Catholic Register*. Retrieved October 10, 2008, from http://209.85.173.104/search?q=cache:Epa_tUJWcoIJ:www.ocsta.on.ca/resources/1/Resources/Our%2520Catholic%2520School%2520Kit/Resource%2520Material.pdf+catholic+schools+caught+in+a+bind+dixon&hl=en&ct=clnk&cd=1&gl=ca

Dworkin, R. (1977). *Taking rights seriously*. Cambridge: Harvard University Press.

Dworkin, R. M. (1985). *A matter of principle*. Cambridge, MA: Harvard University Press.

Dworkin, R. M. (1987). What is equality? Part 3: The place of liberty. *Iowa Law Review, 73*(1), 1–54.

Education Act, R.S.O. (1990). c. E.2. Retrieved June 4, 2005, from www.canlii.org/on/laws/sta/e-2/

Education Act. (1995). S.S. 1995, c. E-0.2. Retrieved June 3, 2005, from www.canlii.org/sk/laws/sta/e-0.2/

Erikson, E. H. (1950). *Childhood and society*. New York: W. W. Norton & Company.

Essex County (R.C. Separate School Board) v. Porter. (1978). 21 O.R. (2d) 255 (C.A.)

Etzioni, A. (Ed.). (1998). *The essential communitarian reader*. Lanham, MD: Rowman and Littlefield.

Feuerherd, J. (2002). Vatican II 40 Years later: Crafting a vision of bishops' conference, then unmaking it. *National Catholic Reporter*. Retrieved March 30, 2005, from www.natcath.com/NCR_Online/archives/100402/100402m.htm

Fisher, A. (2007). *Bishop Fisher on conscience and authority: "Struggling to recover a Catholic sense."* Retrieved from www.zenit.org/english/

Foley, A., Pollock, D., & Walker, T. (1981, February). Meeting the religious needs of non-Catholic students in Catholic schools. *Momentum*, 22–23.

Ford, W. P. (1997). *The formation of one institution's Catholic identity*. Ed.D. University of St. Thomas (Minnesota).

Foster, C. R. (1982). The faith community as a guiding image for Christian education. In D. E. Miller & J. L. Seymour (Eds.), *Contemporary approaches to Christian education* (pp. 53–71). Nashville: Parthenon Press.

Fowler, J. W. (1981). *Stage of faith: The psychology of human development and the question of meaning*. New York: Harper Collins Publishers.

Fowler, J. W. (1991). The vocation of faith development theory. In J. W. Fowler, K. E. Nipkow, & F. Schweitzer (Eds.), *Stages of faith and religious development: Implications for church, education, and society* (pp. 24–25). New York: The Crossroads Publishing Company.

Fowler, J. W., Nipkow, K. E., & Schweitzer, F. (Eds.). (1991). *Stages of faith and religious development: Implications for church, education, and society*. New York: The Crossroads Publishing Company.

Francis, L. J. (1986, February). Are Catholic schools good for non-Catholics? *The Tablet, 15*.

Francis, L. J., & Gibson, H. M. (2001). Growing up Catholic in a Scottish city: The relationship between denominational identity, denominational schools and attitude towards Christianity among eleven to fifteen year olds. *Catholic Education: A Journal of Inquiry and Practice*, *5*(1), 39–54.

Freud, S. (1923). *The ego and the id* (J. Riviere, Trans.). London: Hogarth.

Geaves, R. (1999). Islam and conscience. In J. Hoose (Ed.), *Conscience in world religions* (pp. 155–175). University of Notre Dame Press.

Gilligan, C. (1982). *In a different voice*. Cambridge, MA: Harvard University Press.

Glaser, B. G. (1992). *Basics of grounded theory analysis: Emergence vs. forcing*. Mill Valley, CA: Sociology Press.

Glaser, B. G. (1998). *Doing grounded theory: Issues and discussions*. Mill Valley, CA: Sociology Press.

Gleesen, G. (2003). Conscience and conversion. *Australian Ejournal of Theology*. Retrieved September 22, 2007, from http://dlibrary.acu.edu.au/research/theology/ejournal/aet_1/GGleeson.htm

Gonzalez, R. (2002, November 4). Bishops continue to oppose shared school facilities: Government official says province is not forcing the issue. *Western Catholic Reporter*. Retrieved October 20, 2008, from www.wcr.ab.ca/news/2002/1104/facilities110402.shtml

Gorsky, J. (1999). Conscience in Jewish tradition. In J. Hoose (Ed.), *Conscience in world religions* (pp. 129–154). Notre Dame, IN: University of Notre Dame Press.

Grajczonek, J., Ryan, M., & Chambers, M. (2007). Inclusion of Students who are not Catholics in Catholic Schools: Policy, Practices and Problems. A paper presented at The Fourth International Conference on Catholic Educational Leadership, 29 July - 1 August 2007 in Sydney, Australia. Retrieved March 5, 2009 from http://www.acu.edu.au/__data/assets/pdf_file/0004/89896/Inclusion_of_Students_who_are_not_Catholics_in_Catholic_Schools.pdf

Greeley, A. M. (2002). *Catholic high schools and minority students*. New Brunswick, NJ: Transaction Publishers.

Green, J. (2009, March 7). 'Diversity' is the watchword at today's Catholic schools, where 32 per cent of students aren't Catholic. The Star Phoenix. Retrieved March 12, 2009 from http://www.thestarphoenix.com/Life/pray+same/1364893/story.html

Grisez, G. (1983). *The way of the Lord Jesus, Vol. 1. Christian moral principles*. Chicago: Franciscan Herald Press.

Grisez, G. (1999). The duty and right to follow one's judgment of conscience. In C. E. Curren & R. A. McCormick (Eds.), *The historical development of fundamental moral theology in the United States* (pp. 267–281). Mahwah, NJ: Paulist Press. [Originally published in Linacre Quarterly 56 (February 1989)]

Groome, T. H. (1996). What makes a school Catholic? In T. H. Mclaughlin, J. M. O'Keefe, & B. O'Keeffe (Eds.), *The contemporary Catholic school: Context, identity and diversity* (pp. 107–125). London, Washington: Falmer.

Groome, T. H. (1998). *Educating for life: A spiritual vision for every teacher and parent.* Allen, TX: Thomas More.

Gutmann, A., & Thompson, D. (1990). Moral conflict and political consensus. In R. B. Douglass, G. M. Mara, & H. S. Richardson (Eds.), *Liberalism and the good* (pp. 125–147). New York: Routledge.

Gwynne v. Canada (Minister of Justice). 37 W.C.B. (2d) 355 (British Columbia Court of Appeal, 1998).

Hall (Litigation Guardian of) v. Powers. (2002). 213 D.L.R. (4th) 308 (Ont. SCJ). Retrieved October 10, 2008, from www.canlii.org/en/on/onsc/doc/2002/2002canlii49475/2002canlii49475.html

Halstead, J. (1986). *Conscience, the American bishops and the renewal of moral theology: The notion of conscience in the pastoral letters of the American bishops.* S.T.D. Dissertation, University of Louvain.

Haring, B. (1963). *The law of Christ: Moral theology for priests and laity* (E. G. Kaiser, Trans.). Newman Press. (Originally published 1954)

Haring, B. (1970). *A theology of protest.* Toronto: Doubleday.

Haring, B. (1978). *Free and faithful in Christ: Moral theology for clergy and laity* (Vol. 1). New York: Seabury.

Harkness, T. (n.d.). Authentic and Inclusive Catholic Schools: Some Challenging Contexts. Retrieved March 4, 2009 from http://dlibrary.acu.edu.au/research/theology/ejournal/Issue3/Harkness.htm

Harris, J. (1998). *The nurture assumption: Why children turn out the way they do.* New York: Touchstone Book: Simon & Schuster.

Harvey, P. H. (1994). Crisis and tradition in veritatis spendor. *Studies in Christian Ethics, 7*(2), 1–7.

Haas, J. (2007). Forward. In J. Ratzinger (Ed.), *On conscience: Two essays by Joseph Ratzinger* (pp. 11–41). San Francisco: Ignatius Press.

Hawker, J. F. (1982, February). Arousing the beginnings of faith: The non-Catholic in the Catholic school. *Momentum*, 28–30.

Hawker, R. J. (1987). Schools as an evangelizing community: Guidelines regarding teachers, pupils, parents. In National Catholic Educational Association, *The non-Catholic in the Catholic school* (2nd ed., pp. 1–19). Washington, DC: National Catholic Educational Association.

Hickey, C. T. (1983). *The impact of non-Catholic students in the Catholic schools of a large eastern diocese*. EdD Dissertation, Fordham University UMI 8326176.

Hill, B. V. (1999). Can religious education be theologically neutral? *Journal of Christian Education, 42*(1), 9–24.

Hobbes, T. (1651). *Leviathan.* Retrieved March 5, 2007, from http://etext.library.adelaide.edu.au/h/h681

Hollenbach, D. (1996). The common good, pluralism and Catholic education. In T. H. Mclaughlin, J. M. O'Keefe, & B. O'Keeffe (Eds.), *The contemporary Catholic school: Context, identity and diversity* (pp. 89–103). London, Washington: Falmer.

Hoose, J. (1999). Conscience in the Roman Catholic tradition. In J. Hoose (Ed.), *Conscience in world religions* (pp. 62–98). Notre Dame, IN: University of Notre Dame Press.

International Herald Tribune: Europe. (2007, December 13). Retrieved from www.iht.com/articles/ap/2007/12/13/europe/EU-GEN-Ireland-Immigrant-Schools.php

Jelinski, T. J. (1994). *Admission policies: Catholic divisions in Saskatchewan.* Unpublished Masters Project, University of Saskatchewan, Saskatoon, Saskatchewan.

John Paul II. (1979). *Catechesi tradendae* (On Catechesis in Our Time). In A. Flannery (Ed.), The Vatican collection Vatican II, Vol. 2: More post conciliar documents (Rev. ed., pp. 762–814). Newport, NY: Costello Publishing Company, Inc. Retrieved March 5, 2009 from http://www. vatican.va/holy_father/john_paul_ii/apost_exhortations/documents/hf_jp-ii_exh_16101979_catechesi-tradendae_en.html

John Paul II. (1980, November 14). On the Value and Content of Freedom of Conscience and of Religion. Retrieved Match 9, 2009 from http://www.vatican.va/holy_father/john_paul_ii/messages/pont_messages/1980/documents/hf_jp-ii_mes_19800901_helsinki-act_en.html

John Paul II. (1986, October 27). Pastoral Visit to Perugla and Assisi; Address of John Paul II to the Representatives of the Christian Churches and Ecclesial Communities and of the World Religions. Retrieved October 20, 2008, from www.vatican.va/holy_father/john_paul_ii/speeches/1986/ October/documents/hf_jp-ii_spe_19861027_prayer-peace-assisi-final_en.html

John Paul II. (1988). *Sollicitudo Rei Socialis* (On Social Concerns). Boston: Daughters of St. Paul.

Retrieved March 5, 2009 from http://www.vatican.va/holy_father/john_paul_ii/encyclicals/documents/hf_jp-ii_enc_30121987_sollicitudo-rei-socialis_en.html

John Paul II. (1993). *Veritatis splendor* (The Splendor of Truth). Retrieved September 30, 2006, from www.vatican.va/holy_father/john_paul_ii/encyclicals/documents/hf_jp-ii_enc_06081993_veritati s-splendor_en.html

John Paul II. (1998). *Fides et Ratio* (On the Relationship Between Faith and Reason). Retrieved May 8, 2006, from www.vatican.va/holy_father/john_paul_ii/encyclicals/documents/hf_jp-ii_enc_15101998_fides-et-ratio_en.html

Joyce, J. (1998). *Ulysses* (J. Johnson, Ed.). Oxford: Oxford University Press. (Original work published 1922)

Keys, N. M. (2006). *Aquinas, Aristotle, and the promise of the common good.* New York: Cambridge University Press.

Kohlberg, L. (1981). *Essays on moral development: The philosophy of moral development* (Vol. I). San Francisco: Harper & Row.

Kronman, A. (1996). Leontius' tale. In P. Brooks & P. Gewirtz (Eds.), *Law's stories: Narrative and rhetoric in the law* (pp. 54–56). New Haven: Yale University Press.

Kymlicka, W. (1990). *Contemporary political philosophy: An introduction.* Oxford, UK: Oxford University Press.

Kymlicka. (2002). *Contemporary political philosophy* (2nd ed.). New York: Oxford University Press.

Lacan, J. (1964). *The four fundamental concepts of psycho-analysis.* London: Hogarth Press.

Langan, J. (1990). Catholicism and liberalism: Two hundred years of contest and consensus. In R. B. Douglass, G. M. Mara, & H. S. Richardson (Eds.), *Liberalism and the good* (pp. 105–123). New York: Routledge.

Leal, D. (1999). Against conscience: A protestant view. In J. Hoose (Ed.), *Conscience in world religions* (pp. 21–61). University of Notre Dame Press.

Levinas, E. (1972). *Humanism de l'autre homme.* Fata Morgana.

Löffler, K. (1912). Syncretism. In *The Catholic encyclopedia.* New York: Robert Appleton Company. Retrieved October 3, 2008, from New Advent www.newadvent.org/cathen/14383c.htm

Loder, J. E. (1998). *The transforming moment* (2nd ed.). Colorado Springs, CO: Helmers and Howard Publishers, Inc.

MacIntyre, A. (1981). *After virtue: A study in moral theory.* London: Duckworth.

Maher, M., & Bolland, J. (1912). Soul. *The Catholic encyclopedia.* New York: Robert Appleton Company. Retrieved May 31, 2008, from New Advent www.newadvent.org/cathen/14153a.htm

Maritain, J. (1962). *The education of man.* Garden City, NJ: Doubleday.

Maurice v. Canada (Attorney General). (2002). 210 D.L.R. (4th) 186 (Fed. Ct. Trial Div.). Retrieved September 15, 2007, from www.canlii.org/en/ca/fct/doc/2002/2002fct69/2002fct69.html

May, W. E. (2003). Knowledge, connatural. In Berand L. Marthaler (Ed.), *New Catholic encyclopedia* (2nd ed., Vol. 8, pp. 228–229).

McDonald, D. (2004). Pluralism and public policy: Catholic schools in the United States. In T. C. Hunt, E. A. Joseph, & R. J. Nuzzi (Eds.), *Handbook of research on Catholic education* (pp. 205–228). Greenwich, CT: Information Age Publishing.

McKay, A. G. (2002). The Catholic option: Non-Catholic parents' choice of a religious education in Saskatoon catholic schools. MEd Thesis, University of Saskatchewan. Retrieved March 4, 2009 from http://library2.usask.ca/theses/available/etd-07152008-111457/

McLachlin, B. (2005). Unwritten constitutional principles: What is going on? December 1, 2005 Lord Cooke Lecture, Wellington, New Zealand. Retrieved from http://www.scc-csc.gc.ca/aboutcourt/judges/speeches/UnwrittenPrinciples_e.asp

McLaughlin, T. H. (1996). The distinctiveness of Catholic education. In T. H. Mclaughlin, J. M. O'Keefe, & B. O'Keeffe (Eds.), *The contemporary Catholic school: Context, identity and diversity* (pp. 136–154). London, Washington: Falmer.

Mill, J. S. (1975). *Three essays*. Oxford: Oxford University Press. (Original published 1859)

Miller, P. N. (1996, February). Defining the common good: Empire, religion and philosophy in eighteenth-century Britain. *The American Historical Review*, *101*(1), 179–180.

Minow, M. (1996). Stories in the law. In P. Brooks & P. Gewirtz (Eds.), *Law's stories; Narrative and rhetoric in the law* (pp. 24–36). New Haven, CT: Yale University Press.

Morgan, D. (2001). *Letter on behalf of the Saskatoon Public School Board to the Honorable Jim Melenchuk, Minister of Education, the Province of Saskatchewan.* Retrieved May 6, 2005, from members.shaw.ca/necollegiate/correspondence/letter_to_melenchuk_oct9_01.pdf

Morgan, D. L. (1997). Focus groups as qualitative research. In J. V. Maanen, P. K. Manning, & M. L. Miller (Series Eds.), *Qualitative research methods series* (2nd ed., Vol. 16, pp. 1–80). Newbury Park, CA: Sage.

Mulligan, J. (1999). *Catholic education: The future is now*. Toronto: Novalis.

National Catholic Education Commission [Australia]. (n.d.) Retrieved from www.ncec.catholic.edu.au/pages/index.asp

National Catholic Education Commission (2008). Catholic School Enrollment Trends 2007. Report from the Australian Catholic Education Statistics (ACES) Working Group. Retrieved March 5, 2009 from http://www.ncec.catholic.edu.au/pages/images/Enrolment%20Trends%202007%20(2)7.pdf

National Conference of Catholic Bishops. (1976). *Teach them*. Washington, DC: District of Columbia.

National Conference of Catholic Bishops. (1979). *Sharing the Light of Faith: National Catechetical directory for Catholics in the United States*. Washington, DC: District of Columbia.

Newton, P.M. (n.d.). Separate school divisions. In *The encyclopedia of Saskatchewan*. Retrieved October 10, 2008, from http://esask.uregina.ca/entry/separate_school_divisions.html

Noddings, N. (1984). *Caring: A feminine approach to ethics and moral education*. Berkeley, CA: University of California Press.

Noddings, N. (1998–1999). Longing for the sacred in schools: A conversation with Nel Noddings. *Educational Leadership*. December 1998/January 1999, *56*(4), 28–32. Retrieved June 6, 2005, from www.ascd.org/ed_topics/el199812_halford.html

Nozick, R. (1974). *Anarchy, state, and utopia*. New York: Basic Books.

Nuzzi, R. J. (2004a). Sacred church documents: The organization of centralized authority in Catholic educational administration. In T. C. Hunt, E. A. Joseph, & R. J. Nuzzi (Eds.), *Handbook of research on Catholic education* (pp. 1–25). Greenwich, CT: Information Age Publishing.

Nuzzi, R. J. (2004b). Spirituality and religious education. In T. C. Hunt, E. A. Joseph, & R. J. Nuzzi (Eds.), *Handbook of research on Catholic education* (pp. 65–82). Greenwich, CT: Information Age Publishing.

O.E.C.T.A. v. Ontario (Attorney General) S.C.J. No. 14, 2001 SCC 15 (S.C.C.) (2001), affirming (1999), (sub nom. *Ontario English Catholic Teachers' Association* v. *Ontario (Attorney General)* 44 O.R. (3d) 7 (Ont. C.A.), reversing in part (1998), 162 D.L.R. (4th) 257 (Ont. Gen. Div.)

O'Keefe, J. M. (1997). *Toward a rationale for religiously diverse Catholic schools in the inner cities of the United States*. Retrieved May 30, 2005, from www.shu.edu/catholiced/okeefe.html

Olser, F. (1991a). The development of religious judgement. In F. Olser & W. G. Scarlett (Eds.), *Religious development in child-hood and adolescence* (pp. 5–25). San Francisco: Jossey-Bass, Inc.

Olser, F. (1991b). A logic of religious development. In J. W. Fowler, K. E. Nipkow, & E. Schweitzer (Eds.), *Stages of faith and religious development: Implications for church, education, and society* (pp. 37–64). New York: Crossroad.

Olser, F., & Gmünder, P. (1991). *Religious judgement: A developmental approach*. Birmingham, AL: Religious Education Press.

Ontario Catholic School Trustees Association. (2000). *Our Catholic schools & their future*. Toronto: Ontario Catholic School Trustees' Association.
Ontario Conference of Catholic Bishops. (1993). *Fulfilling the promise: The challenge of leadership*. A Pastoral Letter to the Catholic Education Community. Retrieved from www.occb.on.ca/english/ documents.php?f=fulfilling.html
Oxaal, Z. (2003). In "Second-Guessing the Bishop: Section 93, the Charter, and the 'Religious Government Actor' in the Gay Prom Date Case," 66 *Saskatchewan Law Review* 445.
Palestini, R. H. (2004). *Catholic school administration: Theory, practice, leadership*. Lancaster, PA: ProActive Publications.
Palmieri, A. (1911). Nihilism. In *The Catholic encyclopedia*. New York: Robert Appleton Company. Retrieved October 19, 2008, from New Advent: www.newadvent.org/cathen/11074a.htm
Penn, E. (1985). *A study of non-Catholic parents who enrol their children in Catholic secondary schools*. EdD Dissertation, University of Cincinnati, University Microfilms International. UMI 8518111.
Pettkus v Becker 117 DLR (3d) 257, pp. 92–94 (S.C.C.) (1980). Retrieved August 15, 2007, from http://www.canlii.org/eliisa/highlight.do?text=Pettkus+v+Becker+&language=en&searchTitle=Advanced+Search&path=/en/ca/scc/doc/1980/1980canlii22/1980canlii22.html
Piaget, J. (1932). *The moral judgment of the child*. London: Routledge.
Potts, T. (1980). *Conscience in medieval philosophy*. Cambridge: Cambridge University Press.
R. v. Big M Drug Mart Ltd. (1985). 1 S.C.R. 295. Retrieved September 25, 2007, from http://scc.lexum.umontreal.ca/en/1985/1985rcs1-295/1985rcs1-295.html
R. v. Morgentaler 1 S.C.R. 30. (1998). Retrieved September 25, 2007, from http://scc.lexum.umontreal. ca/en/1988/1988rcs1-30/1988rcs1-30.html
Raddell, W. J. (2000). The challenge of teaching religion in Catholic schools. In T. C. Hunt, T. E. Oldenski, & T. J. Wallace (Eds.), *Catholic school leadership: An invitation to lead* (pp. 105–112). London: Falmer Press.
Rathwell v. Rathwell 2 S.C.R. 436 (1978). Retrieved September 25, 2007, from http://www.canlii.org/ en/ca/scc/doc/1978/1978canlii3/1978canlii3.html
Ratzinger, J. (1969). The dignity of the human person (W. J. O'Hara, Trans.). In H. Vorgrimler (Ed.), *Commentary of the documents of Vatican II, Vol. 5, pastoral constitution of the church in the modern world (Gaudium et Spes)* (pp. 115–163). Montreal, Quebec: Palm Publishers. [Original edition: *Das Zweite Vatikanische Konzilg Dokumente und Kommentare. Part III*, Herder, Freiburg, 1986 (pp. 241–592)]
Ratzinger, J. (1996a). *Salt of the earth: The Church at the end of the millennium (An interview with Peter Seewald)*. Francisco: Ignatius Press.
Ratzinger, J. (1996b). *Relativism: The central problem for faith today*. An address during the meeting of the Congregation for the Doctrine of the Faith with the presidents of the Doctrinal Commissions of the Bishops' Conferences of Latin America held in Guadalajara, Mexico, May. Retrieved June 30, 2005, from www.ewtn.com/library/CURIA/RATZRELA.HTM
Ratzinger, J. (2007). *On conscience: Two essays by Joseph Ratzinger*. San Francisco: Ignatius Press.
Ratzinger, J., & Messori, V. (1985). *The Ratzinger report: An exclusive interview on the state of the Church*. San Francisco: Ignatius Press.
Rawls, J. (1971). *A theory of justice*. London: Oxford University Press.
Rawls, J. (1987). The idea of an overlapping consensus. *Oxford Journal of Legal Studies, 7*, 1–25.
Rawls, J. (1988). Priority of right and ideas of the good. *Philosophy and Public Affairs, 17*, 251–276.
Richardson, H. S. (1990). The problem of liberalism and the good. In R. B. Douglass, G. M. Mara, & H. S. Richardson (Eds.), *Liberalism and the good* (pp. 1–28). London: Routledge.
Robbins, M. (1978). *Conscience in Protestant ethics: An examination of Protestant views of the nature and function of conscience focusing on the thought of select contemporary theologians*. Photocopy, Ann Arbor, Mich.: University microfilms, 1979. PhD Thesis, Emory University. Archived at OCLC's Experiment Thesis Catalogue (U.S.A.).

Roche, K. (1996, October). "Creative insubordination" Catholic school studies. *A Journal of Education for Australian and New Zealand Catholic schools*, *9*(2), 45–46.
Rodriguez v. British Columbia (Attorney General). (1993). 107 D.L.R. (4th) 342 (S.C.C.). Retrieved September 15, 2007, from http://scc.lexum.umontreal.ca/en/1993/1993rcs3-519/1993rcs3-519.html
Rousseau, J.-J. (1980). *Reveries of a solitary walker* (P. France, Trans.). London: Penguin Books. (Original work published 1782)
Rummery, G. (2001). *Catechesis and religious education in a pluralist society*. Keynote address Second National Symposium on Religious Education and Ministry, Sancta Sophia College, Sydney, Australia. Retrieved May 28, 2005, from http://203.10.46.30/mre/symp/index.html#about
Sandel, M. (1982). *Liberalism and the limits of justice*. Cambridge: Cambridge University Press.
Saskatchewan Board of Education. (2001, October 9). *Letter to the Saskatchewan Minister of Education*. Retrieved May 6, 2005, from members.shaw.ca/necollegiate/ correspondence/ letter_to_ melenchuk_oct9_01.pdf
Saskatchewan Ministers of Education. (2001). *Letter from the board of education*. Retrived May 6, 2005, from shaw.ca/necollegiate/correspondence/letter_to_melenchuk_oct9_01.pdf
Satre, J.-P. (1964). *Nausea* (L. Alexander, Trans.). New York: New Directions.
Scannell, T. (1909). Christian doctrine. In *The Catholic encyclopedia*. New York: Robert Appleton Company. Retrieved October 26, 2008, from New Advent: www.newadvent.org/cathen/05075b.htm
School Act, R.S.A. (2000). c. S-3 Retrieved June 4, 2005, from www.canlii.org/ab/laws/sta/s-3/20050617/whole.html
School Admissions Code of Practice. (2003, February). Section 3.10. Retrieved April 4, 2008, from http://64.233.167.104/search?q=cache:GtAVZieQvYQJ:www.dfes.gov.uk/sacode/docs/DFES-school%2520Admissions.pdf+The+British+Department+for+Education+new+Schools+Admission+Code&hl=en&ct=clnk&cd=3&gl=ca
Schillo, G. (1980, April). *Non-Catholics in Catholic schools: A challenge to evangelization*. Paper presented at the 77th annual meeting of the National Catholic Educational Association, New Orleans, LA, April 7–10, 1980.
Schwandt, T. A. (2007). *The sage dictionary of qualitative inquiry: Third edition*. Los Angeles: Sage.
Seeley, S. R. (2000). *Non-Catholic students in a Catholic secondary school: A participatory study*. EdD Dissertation, University of San Francisco Faculty of Education. UMI 9968218.
Selznick, P. (1986, March 5). *The idea of a communitarian morality*. Valedictory lecture. Berkeley, CA: Department of Sociology, University of Columbia.
Sharma, A. (2004). *Hinduism and human rights: A conceptual approach*. Oxford: Oxford University Press.
Shimabukuro, G. (2004). A role analysis based on church documents, dissertations, and recent research. In T. C. Hunt, E. A. Joseph, & R. J. Nuzzi (Eds.), *Handbook of research on Catholic education* (pp. 125–146). Greenwich, CT: Information Age Publishing.
Smart, N. (1968). *Secular education and the logic of religion*. New York: Humanities Press.
Smith, A. (1904). *An inquiry into the nature and causes of the wealth of nations* (2 Vols.). Everyman's Library. London: Dent & Sons. (Original published 1776)
Smith, R. J. (1998). *Conscience and Catholicism: The nature and function of conscience in contemporary Roman Catholic moral theology*. Lanham, MD: University of America, Inc.
Smith, W. J., Foster, W. F., & Donahue, H. M. (1999, Fall). Transformation of educational governance in Quebec: A reform whose time has finally come. *McGill Journal of Education, 207*.
Soulos *v*. Korkontzilas 2 S.C.R. 217. (1997). Retrieved September 19, 2007, from http://scc.lexum.umontreal.ca/en/1997/1997rcs2-217/1997rcs2-217.html
Statement of Conclusions for Meeting of Australian Bishops and the Prefects and Secretaries of Six Dicasteries of the Roman Curia. (1998). Retrieved October 20, 2008, from www.vatican.va/roman_curia/congregations/ccdds/documents/rc_con_ccdds_doc_20000630_ dichiarazione-vescovi-australiani%20_lt.html

Steinwachs, V. (1994, February-March). Planting the seeds of ecumenism: The growing number of other-than-Catholic students and teachers in our schools offers an opportunity for the appreciation of other faith traditions. *Momentum*, 51–53.

Strauss, A., & Corbin J. (1998). *Basics of qualitative research: Techniques and procedures for developing grounded theory* (2nd ed.). Thousand Oaks, CA: Sage.

St. Thomas Aquinas. (2006). Lectura Romana in Primum Sententiarum Petri Lombardi, dist. 38, Q. 2, art. 4. In J. F. Boyle & L. E. Boyle (Eds.).

Sullivan, W. M. (1990). Bringing the good back. In R. B. Douglass, G. M. Mara, & H. S. Richardson (Eds.), *Liberalism and the good* (pp. 148–166). New York: Routledge.

Suresh v. Canada (Minister of Citizenship and Immigration) 1 S.C.R. 3. (2002). Retrieved September 19, 2007, from http://scc.lexum.umontreal.ca/en/2002/2002scc1/2002scc1.html

Swan, M. (2007, May 10). Catholic schools under fire. *The Catholic Register*. Retrieved May 3, 2008, from www.catholicregister.org/content/view/692/849/

Taylor, C. (1979). What's wrong with negative liberty. In A. Ryan (Ed.), *The idea of freedom: Essays in honour of Isaiah Berlin* (pp. 175–194). Oxford: Oxford University Press.

Taylor, C. (1989). Cross-purposes: The liberal-communitarian debate. In N. L. Rosenblum (Ed.), *Liberalism and the moral life* (pp. 159–182). Cambridge, MA: Harvard University Press.

Taylor, C. (1995). *Philosophical arguments*. Cambridge, MA: Harvard University Press.

The Catechism of the Catholic Church. (1992). Retrieved January 8, 2007, from www.vatican.va/archive/catechism/ccc_toc.htm

The Code of Canon Law (in English Translation). (1983). *London, Collins liturgical publication*. Retrieved September 25, 2007, from www.vatican.va/archive/ENG1104/_INDEX.HTM

The British North America Act, 1867. Statutes of Great Britain. (1867). 30 & 31 Victoria, Chap. 3. Retrieved October 12, 2007, from http://home.cc.umanitoba.ca/~sprague/bna.htm

The religious dimension of education in a Catholic school, a document of the sacred congregation for Catholic education, Rome. (1988). Ottawa, ON: The Canadian Conference of Catholic Bishops Publications.

Thomas, S. (1999). Conscience in orthodox thought. In J. Hoose (Ed.), *Conscience in world religions* (pp. 99–125). Notre Dame, IN: University of Notre Dame Press.

Tonnies, F. (1955). *Gemeinschaft und Gesellschaft* (C. Loomis, Trans.). London: Routeledge & Kegan Paul Ltd. (Original work published 1887)

Twinning, W. (1997). Civilians don't try: A comment on Mirjan Damaska's "Rational and Irrational Proof Revisited" (1997). 5 Cardozo J. Int'l & Comp. L. 69 at fn. 6.

United States Conference of Catholic Bishops. (1972). *To teach as Jesus did: A pastoral message on Catholic education*. Washington, DC: District of Columbia.

United States Conference of Catholic Bishops. (2005). *Renewing our commitment to Catholic elementary and secondary schools in the third millennium*. Washington, DC: District of Columbia.

United States v. Burns 1 S.C.R. 283. (2001). Retrieved September 19, 2007, from http://scc.lexum.umontreal.ca/en/2001/2001scc7/2001scc7.html

Vatican II. (1964a, November 21). *Lumen Gentium (Dogmatic Constitution of the Church)*. Retrieved October 20, 2008, from www.vatican.va/archive/hist_councils/ii_vatican_council/documents/vat-ii_const_19641121_lumen-gentium_en.html

Vatican II. (1964b, November 21). *Unitatis Redintegratio (Decree On Ecumenism)*. Retrieved October 20, 2008, from www.vatican.va/archive/hist_councils/ii_vatican_council/documents/vat-ii_decree_19641121_unitatis-redintegratio_en.html

Vatican II. (1965a). *Dignitatis Humanae* (Declaration On Religious Liberty: On the Right of the Person and of Communities to Social and Civil Freedom in Matters Religious). In A. Flannery (Ed.), *The basic sixteen documents Vatican II: Constitutions decrees declarations* (pp. 551–568). Newport, NY: Costello Publishing Company, Inc. Retrieved May 6, 2006, from www.vatican.va/archive/hist_councils/ii_vatican_council/documents/vat-ii_decl_19651207_dignitatis-humanae_en.html

Vatican II. (1965b). *Gravissimum educationis (Declaration on Christian Education)*. Retrieved September 30, 2007, from www.vatican.va/archive/hist_councils/ii_vatican_council/documents/vat-ii_decl_19651028_gravissimum-educationis_en.html

Vatican II. (1965c, December 7). *Gaudium Et Spes (Pastoral Constitution on the Church in the Modern World)*. Retrieved Octover 10, 2008, from www.vatican.va/archive/hist_councils/ii_vatican_council/documents/vat-ii_cons

Vaughn, S. (1996). *Focus group interviews in education and psychology*. Thousand Oaks, CA: Sage.

Walker, L. (1911). Relativism. In *The Catholic encyclopedia*. New York: Robert Appleton Company. Retrieved October 3, 2008, from New Advent www.newadvent.org/cathen/12731d.htm

Wallace, T. J. (2000). We are called: The principal as faith leader in the Catholic school. In T. C. Hunt, T. E. Oldenski, & T. J. Wallace (Eds.), *Catholic school leadership* (pp. 191–203). New York: Falmer Press.

Wilson, J. (2007, September 17). *Faith based schools: How provincial governments finance religious schools*. CBCNews.ca. Retrieved May 2, 2008, from www.cbc.ca/ontariovotes2007/features/ features-faith.html

Wolf, S. (1992). Comment. In A. Gutmann (Ed.), *Multiculturalism and the politics of recognition. An essay by Charles Taylor* (pp. 75–86). Princeton, NJ: Princeton Univeristy Press.

Yellowknife Catholic Schools v. Euchner. (2007). *NWTSC 15*. Retrieved August 4, 2007, from http://www.canlii.org/en/nt/ntsc/doc/2007/2007nwtsc15/2007nwtsc15.html See also: www.cbc.ca/ canada/north/story/2007/05/25/catholic-court.html See also the Appeal Decision (2008) Retrieved March 8, 2009 at : http://www.canlii.org/en/nt/ntca/doc/ 2008/2008nwtca13/2008nwtca13.html

Zenit. (2007, June 18). *Spirit of Assisi is not syncretism affirms Pope: Says it is 'Evangelical' to unite acceptance and faith*. Retrieved October 10, 2008, from www.zenit.org/article-19914?l=english

Zenit. (2006, February 10). *Catholic schools and non-Catholic students: Interview with director of St. Dominic's institute of Rome*. Retrieved October 10, 2008, from www.zenit.org/article-15249?l=english

J. KENT DONLEVY

B.A., B.Ed., M.Ed., LL.B, Ph.D.

Dr. Donlevy is the Associate Dean (Interim) of the Graduate Division of Educational Research in the Faculty of Education at the University of Calgary, in the Province of Albert, Canada, and the Vice-Chair of the University of Calgary's Conjoint Faculties Research Ethics Board. He has taught grades 4-12 (inclusive), been a Catholic school principal, and is permanently certified as a teacher in the Provinces of Alberta and Saskatchewan. He has negotiated on local levels for both the Alberta Teachers' Association and the Saskatchewan Teachers' Federation. He is also a member of the Saskatchewan Law Society, having become a barrister & solicitor in 1985. His contact information is as follows.
Graduate Division of Educational Research
Faculty of Education
University of Calgary
2500 University Drive, N.W.
Calgary, Alberta.
T2N 1N4
Canada
E-mail: donlevy@ucalgary.ca
Tel: 1.403.220-2973
Fax: 1.403.282-3005

#21 ROCKY VISTA Terrace N.W
Calgary T3G5G5

Printed in the United States
146882LV00002B/2/P

9 789087 908058